The Future of the World
Is Open

SUNY series in Contemporary Italian Philosophy

Silvia Benso and Brian Schroeder, editors

The Future of the World Is Open

Encounters with Lea Melandri, Luisa Muraro, Adriana Cavarero, and Rossana Rossanda

Elvira Roncalli

Published by State University of New York Press, Albany

© 2022 State University of New York

All rights reserved

Printed in the United States of America

No part of this book may be used or reproduced in any manner whatsoever without written permission. No part of this book may be stored in a retrieval system or transmitted in any form or by any means including electronic, electrostatic, magnetic tape, mechanical, photocopying, recording, or otherwise without the prior permission in writing of the publisher.

For information, contact State University of New York Press, Albany, NY
www.sunypress.edu

Library of Congress Cataloging-in-Publication Data

Name: Roncalli, Elvira, author.
Title: The future of the world is open : encounters with Lea Melandri,
   Luisa Muraro, Adriana Cavarero, and Rossana Rossanda / Elvira Roncalli.
Description: Albany : State University of New York Press, 2022. | Series:
   SUNY series in contemporary Italian philosophy | Includes bibliographical
   references and index.
Identifiers: LCCN 2022005567 | ISBN 9781438489155 (hardcover : alk. paper) |
   ISBN 9781438489162 (ebook) | ISBN 9781438489148 (pbk. : alk. paper)
Subjects: LCSH: Feminism—Italy. | Feminist theory—Italy. | Women—Italy—
   Social conditions.
Classification: LCC HQ1642 .F88 2022 | DDC 305.42010945—dc23/eng/20220504
LC record available at https://lccn.loc.gov/2022005567

10 9 8 7 6 5 4 3 2 1

A mia madre,
"*For we think back through our mothers if we are women.*"
—Virginia Woolf

Contents

Acknowledgments ix

Introduction 1

Lea Melandri

1. The Memory of Our Body (*La memoria del corpo*):
   In Conversation with Lea Melandri 21

Luisa Muraro

2. "But I Am a Woman": Sexual Difference as Subjective Truth
   ("Ma io sono una donna": *Differenza sessuale come verità soggettiva*): In Conversation with Luisa Muraro 67

Adriana Cavarero

3. An Imaginary of Hope (*Un immaginario di speranza*):
   In Conversation with Adriana Cavarero 113

Rossana Rossanda

4. Selected Essays by Rossana Rossanda 157
   The Unrepentant Emancipated Woman 157
   A Worthy Challenge, an Assured Conflict: Women and the Polis 165
   Care Amiche 169

Notes	175
About the Author	185
Index	187

Acknowledgments

Everyone knows that "many hands" go into a book from start to finish. An idea may arise in the mind of someone as she is teaching, reading, writing, speaking with a colleague, or while doing something entirely "mundane," having little to do—at least directly—with philosophy. But ideas come and go. However interesting, worthwhile and original, an idea is just that, a mere "idea," something intangible, invisible. Unless . . . the conditions are such that the idea can take material shape, thus becoming concrete and visible to others as well. This passage involves "many hands" as it were, and it is to the many whose "hands" helped making this book possible that I turn with a thankful heart.

In its very early stage, this project received the summer Berberet grant from Carroll College Faculty Development Committee. I wish to thank the members of FDC for their diligence in promoting faculty's many endeavors and J. Berberet for instituting the grant and generously sustaining it over the years.

Maria Luisa Boccia was pivotal in connecting me with Tommaso Di Francesco at *Il Manifesto*, and for suggesting Rossana Rossanda's article "L'impenitente emancipata." Thank you, Maria Luisa for your generous and kind assistance in these crucial steps.

I wish to thank Tommaso Di Francesco, co-director of *Il Manifesto*, for his kind permission to publish Rossana Rossanda's articles "Una bella sfida, un conflitto sicuro. Le donne e la polis," and "Care Amiche," both of which first appeared on *Il Manifesto*, and for providing Rossana Rossanda's photo taken by photographer Carlo Leida which appears in this volume. Tommaso Di Francesco also connected me with Tiziana, the archivist of *Il Manifesto*, whose help was invaluable. Thank you, Francesco and Tiziana, for your solicitous and skillful hand.

I wish to thank the anonymous reviewers for their time in reading the manuscript and their attentiveness to every part of it, big and small. Your careful review and your insights revealed ways of reading—and listening to—the conversations I was not fully conscious of, and this, I found most enriching.

I am especially thankful to Michael Rinella, Diane Ganeles, Michael Campochiaro and the staff at SUNY Press, for their editorial competence, their prompt and most adept assistance, as well as their kind and friendly disposition.

My most sincere thanks to Brian Schroeder and Silvia Benso, editors of the SUNY series in Contemporary Italian Philosophy in which this book appears. Their constant support and encouragement have been like a steady hand, always there. To Silvia, in particular, for your expert advice every step of the way, your perseverant attentiveness and inspiring confidence. I am especially thankful for our friendship and the many "meaning-full" conversations.

I wish to thank my editors "in residence," especially "R." for your agility in moving from one language to another and your nimble skills with the riddles of computer programs simply indispensable at some critical junctions. "J." for your meticulous reading and your unfailing support. To both of you, and to the others "in residence" who, with a smile, a word or a freely given opinion, have helped me along the way, *grazie infinite*.

Last but not least, I extend my sincerest and deepest gratitude to Lea Melandri, Luisa Muraro, and Adriana Cavarero for saying "yes" to the idea without a flicker of hesitation. Without your thoughtful consideration of every question, your willingness to meet "virtually" more than once, your attentive reading, as well as your endless patience, this volume would not be. Thank you for making it possible.

Elvira Roncalli

Introduction

This volume gathers conversations with Lea Melandri, Luisa Muraro, and Adriana Cavarero, and essays by Rossana Rossanda—Italian women thinkers and authors whose words give shape to the social, political, and philosophical discussions that arose out of the women's movement of the late 1960s and 1970s in Italy.

The impetus for this project came, in part, from the desire to speak with women whose lives and work have played—and continue to play—an important part in the women's movement and feminist thought in Italy. As a philosophy student at the State University of Milan—*la statale*, as it is commonly known—in the late 1980s and early 1990s, I discovered feminism in and through my friendship with other philosophy students—young women like me—not through the program of studies. The only course I took that focused on a woman thinker was on Hannah Arendt, and that was the exception. When I went to look for books by Arendt at the philosophy library, I could not find any. Hannah Arendt had lived and thought, but none of her books could be found at the State University of Milan in the early 1990s. Things have changed since then and, I have no doubt, many books by Arendt and on Arendt can be found at the Milan University library today. Still, the question of what constitutes knowledge, which books and thinkers become part of the program of studies, and which do not, remains a central question for everyone, especially for anyone involved in teaching and learning. At the time I understood that if I wanted to learn what women philosophers had thought and written, I had to go and look for them myself, and beyond those institutional, academic walls.

When I currently think of my university years in Milan, I think of my friends, the time we spent together, and the intensity of the personal, philosophical, and political discoveries we experienced while together. The courses I took, the books we had to read, the examinations, and everything else that happened in those years fades in the background. I only have flashes of memory of the place, the overly packed classrooms, the courtyards, the philosophy library where I often studied, the coffee shops just outside the university building, the bookstore with its walls and floor stacked with books, and their friendly staff.

I moved away from Italy and the University of Milan, but the scarcity of women thinkers in the main programs of studies in philosophy—unless designated as a specific area of studies such as "gender," "race," and so on—accompanied me wherever I went. As had been the case at *la statale*, what happened outside the classroom—discussion groups and informal reading sessions on books and thinkers not in the program of studies—was as formative as what was learned inside, and perhaps even more so.

The conversations presented in this volume are like the many conversations I have had over the years with friends, colleagues, students in my courses and, in my mind, also with the authors themselves. They are, in many respects, a way of stringing a thread between different times and places, among singular experiences and patterns that seem to return. Even though I am now far away from the time and place of the late 1980s and early 1990s, in other ways it is as if I never left: the desire to engage in conversations inside and outside institutional knowledge continues to animate my desire to understand.

Lea Melandri, Luisa Muraro, and Adriana Cavarero are central figures in Italian feminism and Italian thought. As their lifelong work attests, they have persisted in naming, elaborating, making visible, and detailing women's experience—sexual difference, Muraro prefers to call it—its value, its meaning, and its contradictions. These thinkers belong to a generation of women who "were there" at a time when the women's movement and students' revolt radically questioned the status quo at all levels of Italian society and sought to change it. The extent to which each of them was involved, and the impact that their direct participation had on each of them, on their choices, and on their subsequent work, becomes clear through these conversations and through their own words. In answering the questions that are posed to them, they draw out the main points clearly and directly, thus opening a window onto key aspects of their thought and providing an entry into their way of thinking. They tell us about themselves and their work, or better, they tell us how their work and their thought stem out of concrete events and their own relationships with other women and men.

These conversations are intended to be explorations of Melandri's, Muraro's, and Cavarero's thought where previous familiarity with their respective work is helpful, though not indispensable for appreciating the originality of each. Their words will speak differently to different readers. Still, there is much that they leave for us to think about if only we consider some of the questions they raise: they ask about subjectivity, feminine subjectivity in particular, about the relationship between theory and practice, about the political and what it entails, about change, about knowledge, about naming experience in its manifoldness and finding the right words to say it. These are questions for which I have no clear or definitive answer; but precisely because of that, the questions draw me in and draw me to others.

While the work of Melandri, Muraro, and Cavarero originates in a specific time and place—Italy in the late 1960s and 1970s—it is also true that it is not confined to that time and place, and many will find echoes of these women's words in their own experience and in how they think about it. Perhaps in this lies the urgency of this book: we need to hear from those whose political struggle has given rise to practices and words that have brought about change, even when the cultural context and the time are somewhat distant. Mechanisms of domination are, not surprisingly, monotonous and repetitive; it is on the side of those who struggle to subvert them that political creativity lies. In hearing and learning about these struggles it becomes possible to establish points of contact and even draw a map across time and space that tells us about political struggles in their concrete situations.

In speaking about their work, the three authors speak about their life at the crossroads of events happening in Italy that impacted them directly. The Italian social and political context in the late 1960s and 1970s is not usually well known among English-speaking readers, but it is crucial for understanding the originality—in the double sense of origins and distinctness—of the women's movement and feminism in Italy. Within the limits of this introduction, it is not possible to provide an exhaustive picture of those years.[1] Yet each conversation lets their significance transpire: Melandri, Muraro, and Cavarero refer to the period between the late 1960s and 1970s as a time of profound change. These are tumultuous years in Italy, as they are years of widespread social and political unrest that shook the establishment at its foundations, leaving no state institutions, no main social player untouched: from students' protests in the universities, to workers' strikes in the factories, to teachers' mobilization at all school levels. As workers, as teachers, and as students, women were involved in all of these social and political struggles, but they soon came to realize that their being women did not appear to have any significance, except as something to be "dealt with" from within the overall workers' or students' demands. Historically, however—a history that goes back a long way—being women had had a significant impact on their lives: it had penalized them to a subordinate condition, deprived them of the power to decide for themselves, excluded them from all decision-making powers that regulate living together, reduced them to a condition of total dependence. As it became clear that the specificity of being woman was not central to these rebellious movements, women left them and became a political movement of their own, with their own political goals and their own claims, separate from the other social movements of this period. From their separate position, they began to produce knowledge about their condition as women in a patriarchal culture, and the blow their departure inflicted on "man" was aptly depicted by Carla Lonzi:

> Man no longer knows who woman is when she comes out of her colonization and from her roles through which he was preparing himself for an experience already done and repeated over the millennia: the mother, the virgin, the wife, the lover, the daughter, the sister, the sister-in-law, the female friend, the prostitute. Woman was a product prepackaged in such a way that he had nothing to discover in that human being. Every role presented itself as his guarantee for him himself; to come out of that guarantee was like falling off from man's consideration, it was the end. Every woman who "differs" today knows that every man in his heart decrees her as the end, since, by not being able to catalog her, he feels irritated and powerless having to confront the fact that the understanding between the sexes is no longer so clear.[2]

Carla Lonzi refers to the condition of woman as one of "colonization" and not by accident. A colonized nation is overtaken by the colonizing power and controlled through the imposition of laws, customs, and a language that are not its own. Ultimately, the colonized power is one that takes hold of people and controls them from within. Similarly, a woman in a patriarchal society is the product of a law and of customs that take hold of her from within; she speaks a language that is not her own. To free oneself from any form of colonization entails sorting through the ambiguity and contradictions that permeate one's condition, and it requires a conscientious effort in taking a good look at everything one says and does, trying to find a way to disentangle oneself from what is foreign and what is one's own. Muraro acknowledges the Eurocentric imprint of her educational formation, a given in the sociocultural context of her upbringing, but as a woman, she has to find her way to relate to it, by cultivating "a sense of partiality," looking for the way of symbolic independence from the dominant culture and affirm her subjective truth. Similarly, Melandri wrestles with a "feminine" as "the specter of man's desires and fears," caught in a dualism where woman is the source both of sin and of moral elevation, man's damnation and his salvation. She looks instead for the links between these conceptual oppositions that continue to plague the Western way of thinking even after they have fallen in disrepute.

There is a recurring insistence on a partiality that cannot be subsumed into a universality and that cannot be done away with. It attests to the limits of language and of theory while speaking of the need to transform both language and theory in and through the practices that arise out of the feminist political struggle, knowing all too well that some "betraying" occurs in translating such practices into theory.

In talking about themselves and their work, Melandri, Muraro, and Cavarero all refer to those years as the context wherein each of them experienced a turning point, leading them to a conscious awareness that transformed their respective lives radically. Melandri fled the constraints of a life—a job, a husband—that had already closed her in at the age of twenty-five and found herself in the midst of the anti-authoritarian school movement and the women's movement. Muraro grasped the full import of being a woman when questioned directly by her professor about doing philosophy and about "turning to the feminists." Cavarero realized the power of the imagination in subverting domination through the 1968 students' revolt.

Even though such a turning point takes a slightly different form for each of them, it is evident for all of them that there is a clear sense of "before" and "after," as if a metamorphosis has taken place: she is the same woman, but also no longer the woman she was before. This hiatus becomes an opening for discovering and naming her experience, with her own words and together with the words of other women. It is not surprising that the *pratica di autocoscienza* (consciousness raising)—the practice of gathering and telling one another of their lives as women—was a powerful political tool in the women's movement in Italy. Women, whose existence was not their own, were discovering ways of saying and speaking for themselves, each by herself, in her own words, aided by the words of other women, expressing what had been negated, buried, censored, and discarded. In the words of Melandri: never had women appeared more threatening to the patriarchal order than when they came together and found their own words with which to speak.

Adherence to material experience is one of the threads that runs through their work and something that is found in feminist theory at large, inside and outside Italy. What is less known, however, is that the 1970s women's movement in Italy, although part of a global phenomenon, had its own peculiarities. It was heterogeneous, fairly widespread all over Italy, particularly combative in urban centers, rooted in the practice of *autocoscienza*, and operating through many autonomously self-regulated collectives. The writings produced by these collectives gave rise to animated debates across Italy and would influence the discussions on divorce, on abortion, and on a reform of family law.[3]

Within a substantially similar orientation—adhering to material experience and, from within it, giving words to feminine specificity—Melandri, Muraro, and Cavarero exhibit different ways of proceeding, employing different strategies wherein we get a taste of what could be referred to as "variations on a theme," provided that we understand that "the theme" is not something external but, rather, a fundamental orientation that has come about through a deeply transformative experience. It may be interesting to know that their lives intersect, something that has, no doubt, contributed to this shared orientation. Muraro and Melandri were involved in the anti-authoritarian school movement and in the women's movement in the 1970s, and they both participated in early feminist collectives. Cavarero and Muraro are among the founders of the philosophical community Diotima at the University of Verona in the 1980s. Although they are not working with one another at present, they are nonetheless working closely, or to put it differently, their work is closely related.

The similar orientation notwithstanding, it is important not to lose the specificity of the work of each and the underlining questions that animate it. Melandri focuses on excavating the memory of our bodies and plumbs the region at the threshold between the conscious and the unconscious. Cavarero explores philosophical and literary stereotypes and figures of the past to free them from the patriarchal system of values, thereby making new compositions of value and meaning possible. Muraro finds in sexual difference and in the practice of relationships with other women the path to a symbolic order that empowers women—an order that is centered on the figure of the mother, the source of feminine authority.

Sexual difference is how Muraro and Cavarero talk about feminine specificity, and this cannot be understood as a mere biological category—although this is how it is often mistakenly interpreted—insofar as it has to do with the symbolic: the culturally, conceptually, philosophically, and theologically complex, yet invisible "apparatus" at work in every context through which one seeks to make sense of one's experience in the world. This apparatus is fundamentally patriarchal, rooted in a conception of the relationship between the sexes in which man holds control through codified laws, and where the living together is primarily organized through the division of productive and reproductive labor. As such, rather than furnishing the tools for understanding and making sense of herself as a woman, this order further entrenches woman in a condition of subordination and dependence. The questions she may have about her role and place in society are silenced by what is legitimized as "natural destiny." Cavarero's work exhibits the "fiction" or the "lie" of the patriarchal symbolic and, in dismantling it, she recovers meanings and values that are not reducible to the prevailing symbolic order but belong to another order. Cavarero finds in the narrative style and in literature a wealth of resources that nourish her imaginary, enabling her to undo stereotypes and unearth what lies beneath them. Muraro turns to the relationships with other women of the Milan Women's Bookstore as the source of inspiration and of a knowledge beyond the prevailing and pervasive male order. It is in the context of these practices that the authority of the mother is rediscovered as a way of empowering women and their desires; it also subverts the preordained dependence of women on men. Relying on the authority of the mother means to entrust oneself to another woman for the realization of one's desire, a desire that, in a patriarchal order, would hardly even arise.

Women's relationships are central to the work of Muraro and the Milan Women's Bookstore as well as the philosophical community Diotima in Verona. It is not difficult to see how both of these places and practices have their roots in the collectives of the women's movement in the 1970s. It does not follow, however, that they are the only practices that have evolved out of the women's movement in Italy.

Lea Melandri tells us of her experience of the women's collectives and how this same experience, passing through the "150-hour courses,"[4] led her and other women to the creation of the Libera Università delle Donne (Free University of Women). The practice of learning from one another is at work here too, but the emphasis is on enabling the expression of the many ways of knowing rather than channeling it through technical and specialized languages. It is a knowing that comes about through "experiential writing," by disinhibiting what has remained mute and has sedimented in the memory of our bodies. Only in interrogating the preestablished notion of being male and being female, in searching for the relations that exist in what appears artificially opposed, does the pervasiveness of male domination come to the fore, and only then does the possibility of change arise. What is needed, according to Melandri, is the ruthless capacity to look at the relationship between the sexes and, particularly, at the most intimate of them all, love, as the locus of the most pervasive form of domination, which has enslaved woman, but which has gravely mutilated man as well.

Melandri, Muraro, and Cavarero "were there," I said earlier, but not in the sense that they had a "privileged" position regarding the women's movement or the students' movement, as if by being involved in those events, they might hold the key to their meaning. On the contrary, it is not possible for any one of them to provide us with the overarching view of that period in a comprehensive way. While they were directly involved, they were not alone. Instead, by saying that they "were there," I simply emphasize what each of them, in her own way, has said: that they were profoundly changed by their experience of those events. Muraro speaks of a correspondence between events and herself, a "happy coincidence," she calls it. In talking about "public happiness," Cavarero seems to refer to something similar: the coming together of people at a particular moment expresses a shared impetus that is not there when individuals are isolated. For Melandri, such a correspondence has come "through another person" (*per interposta persona*) through the words of another woman naming what she, Melandri, could not find words for, at least not until then, at which moment, the correspondence does open up and provides words she did not previously have. They each know most intimately what changing and transforming oneself is about, something that by now must feel almost like an impervious presence within.

It might be more difficult to assess to what extent this profound personal transformation has in fact transmuted into the world around them as well, transforming it, if not radically, at least in visible and significant ways. Melandri refers to the well-known slogan "change yourself and change the world," used by feminists and not only by them, emphasizing that slogans such as these and feminism too, risk becoming devoid of meaning if reduced to a mere formula. To be sure, there is something to be said for such a correspondence, some unexplainable turning of events that impacts one's life deeply, something that could not be foreseen and that is not directly retraceable to some personal traits, at least not entirely. The gratitude that Melandri, Muraro, and Cavarero genuinely express regarding how life has opened up to them attests to their humbleness. They acknowledge that while their personal choices matter—and they matter a lot—there is still something else that is difficult to name or pin down—it is like "wonders," Muraro says—and yet there, nonetheless.

Where does Rossana Rossanda fit into this? She was a well-known and influential figure in Italy, a highly respected journalist, a leading thinker in the Italian Communist Party, from which she was expelled in 1969 together with a few others of *Il Manifesto*,[5] a newspaper she cofounded with others. She died in the fall of 2020 and, with her passing, a world has come to an end too: the world of post-WWII Italy, about which she writes in her memoir *La ragazza del secolo scorso* (The girl from the last century).

Rossanda "was there too" during the late 1960s and 1970s, though not as a direct participant in the women's movement, the students' movement, or the workers' movement. Nonetheless, she was involved as a very close, astute, and sympathetic observer. Just to get a sense of her enthusiasm for the events of the time, in May 1968 Rossanda drove to Paris with some friends, on the spur of the moment, to see with her own eyes the "revolution" as it was unfolding. In light of her political experience and acumen, she knew that something of political magnitude was taking place and wrote that these events constituted "a break in history" (*una cesura storica*),[6] and also that "in Italy, 1968 stretched out more than anywhere else and it did not last just for the month of May" (*e in Italia il 1968 si estese più che altrove e non durò un solo maggio*).[7]

Regarding the women's movement, Rossanda always maintained a critical distance while continually engaging in a dialogue with feminists, many of whom were or became her close friends. She belonged to an older generation who came of age during WWII, in a world where affirming oneself as woman meant to take the road of emancipation. When the new feminism made its appearance, she was moved by it and never grew tired of engaging in its quest, sometimes with the indulgence of a mother who knows what is coming, and always with the fervor that incites pressing forward, while forewarning of what lies hidden.

She too talks about a turning point in her life: it was when she became a communist. It was 1943, and most of Italy was under the occupation of the German troops aided by the Fascists of the Saló regime,[8] a difficult and confusing time. As a student of philosophy at the University of Milan, she turned to her highly respected teacher Antonio Banfi. She had just learned he was a communist. She was looking for some way to orient herself, in a world and at a time where everything she had known had collapsed. He gave her a list of books to read, writings by Marx, Lenin, and Laski. She read every one of them and could not put them down. But it was a vision that opened her eyes to the world around her and moved her to take a stand.

As she wrote in *La ragazza del secolo scorso*, on her way home on a tram, one day, she saw three workers: "Worn out with fatigue and, it seemed to me, with wine, disheveled, with rough hands, black nails, their heads dangling on their chest. I had never looked at them, my world was elsewhere, they were other, and what were they? They were fatigue without light, the things of the world I avoided, about which nothing could be done. . . . It was with them that I had to go." (*Sfiniti di fatica e mi parve di vino, malmessi, le mani ruvide, le unghie nere, le teste penzolanti sul petto. Non li avevo mai guardati, il mio mondo era altrove, loro erano altro, che cosa? Erano la fatica senza luce, le cose del mondo che evitavo, sulle quali nulla si poteva. . . . Era con loro che dovevo andare.*) She continues: "In truth it was not a discovery, it was an acknowledgment without further delay." (*In verità non era un scoperta, era una presa d'atto senza più rinvii possibili.*)[9] It was this vision that made her realize she needed to take a stand and shortly thereafter she joined the Resistance against the German troops and the Fascists. This is the moment of "correspondence" between events and her personal life: she became fully conscious of the situation and immediately she took action; she could no longer remain a bystander. Does she also find herself at this very moment? Her answer is unequivocal: "Nor could I have screamed, one day, 'I was there.' I found myself in it." (*Né avrei potuto gridare un giorno 'io c'ero.' Io mi ci sono trovata.*)[10]

It is a remarkable statement that draws out a subtle distinction between "being there" and "finding herself in the midst of it," where in the latter, the accent is placed first and foremost on the events, on what was happening, and less on her own person. Not to undermine the transformative experience of the resistance, but the urgency, as she put it, came from the situation, from what was happening. This gives rise to some key questions that every social and political movement seeking change—including the women's movement—has had to face, and continues to face: If the political movement expresses a correspondence between events and the people involved in it about something that is perceived as needing to change, how is such an inexplicable "correspondence" maintained over time? If the situation—the events, what is happening—plays such a crucial part in getting a political movement going, how can one maintain such a vital connection while situation and events change? In short: How to hold on to the momentum, while everything passes? It is true that a strong political movement for change does not, and probably cannot, last for a long time—either the political goals are achieved and there is no need for it to continue to exist, or if they are only partially achieved or not at all (depending on the kind of institutional opposition they face), they may subside for a time and then resurge. It is both remarkable and perhaps disheartening that the women's movement, the feminist struggle, keeps on. On the one hand, this speaks of the inspiring, persistent determination animating the struggle, the desire to change the structurally unjust ways in which the relationships between the sexes have been conceived and shaped, relationships still rooted in power unbalance and violence; on the other hand, that it should keep on speaks of how deeply entrenched this way of structuring the relationships between the sexes is, and how hard it is to change them because of that.

The women's movement in Italy has morphed since the 1960s and 1970s. Yet it has not subsided, unlike other movements of the same period. It attests both to the need for more change and for the persistence of the women who bring it forth. It seems to me that, beyond the marked differences in their approaches—not to be underestimated—what stands out is that they responded to the challenge. For as simple and perhaps even obvious this may seem, it should not be taken for granted. For there to be any change at all, the challenge must be taken up. Again, and again.

I wish to say a few words about the modality of these interviews/conversations. Each was carried out separately and independently. I prepared the questions in advance to reflect the specificity of the work of each of the authors. Melandri, Muraro, and Cavarero were asked to respond to the questions in writing. Given travel restrictions imposed by the COVID-19 pandemic, my planned meeting with each of them happened online, and during our "virtual encounters" we had the opportunity to talk about these questions more in-depth, clarifying key points. I was also able to ask more pointed questions based on their initial responses, and the changes that emerged from the "live" conversations were integrated into a final written text. Once I completed the translation from Italian into English, additional revisions were made in concert with each of the interviewees. Through the many back-and-forth exchanges, I came to realize that my way of looking at these texts had changed: I could no longer see them merely as "interviews"; they felt more like conversations, happening across time zones and across space, but conversations nonetheless, where we sought points of contact and through which much of what is not immediately apparent in their work came through.

My "closeness" to them is undeniable; it lies primarily in my genuine curiosity for the work of women—thinkers, authors, writers—and in being moved by the unending quest for finding sense and making sense of our experience as women. This, however, does not entail sameness in thinking; nor does it turn into an uncritical attitude. The conversations show that it is not possible to reduce the work of one to the work of the other, not even of those within a similar orientation; the specificity of each is undeniable. Feminism itself, as a movement and as thought, is not univocal, and even when we look for its defining characteristics within a particular social and cultural context, such as Italy for instance, it remains difficult to find a formula that adequately encapsulates it. Thinking and acting politically always entails many sides.

Rossana Rossanda is part of this, and yet she is apart. As a woman, and a feminist, a reluctant feminist perhaps, she fiercely defended her independence of thought while constantly challenging what she saw as "questionable" or "unconvincing." In the initial stage of this project, I had hoped to be able to interview her as well, but this plan did not materialize, unfortunately. I am delighted to be able to include three of her essays in this volume. They attest to her genuine engagement with feminism, to another voice within the same struggle, and help recreate the atmosphere of intense and lively debate of the time.

The order in which the conversations appear in this volume was not decided in advance. It became manifest in light of the content each thinker brought to light. Lea Melandri tells us a lot about the social movements of the late 1960s and early 1970s in Italy, furnishing a detailed picture of those restless years and of the historical and cultural context. Luisa Muraro speaks of the political practices of the women's movement collectives that coalesced around the Milan Women's Bookstore and that elaborated the thought of sexual difference. Adriana Cavarero's work exemplifies the philosophical elaboration, from within the academy, of key issues and experiences that the women's movement and the thought of sexual difference have brought to the fore. Rossana Rossanda is the voice speaking from without, but participating in thinking about the woman condition, nonetheless. Although she may be viewed as representing a world that was radically put into question at the time of the women's movement, she is, as she puts it, "in the middle of the ford," but precisely for that looking to all sides and calling for an open and sincere dialogue, an invitation to listen to each other "free" from respective affiliations, a conciliatory gesture that inspires new beginnings.

As these conversations took place while the COVID-19 pandemic was spreading, it was impossible not to talk about its impact. The pandemic has made existing inequities all the more visible and when it comes to relationship between the sexes, it has revealed that there is still a lot of work to be done. With regard to political power, women's representation in government and in key decision-making positions still remains low, as Cavarero points out; with the burden of domestic labor and child rearing (still!) falling predominantly on women's backs—and not only in Italy—many women have had to make the difficult decision of leaving their jobs, even when they are very well-paying jobs. In a strange sort of way, what feminists of the 1970s fought for—a more inclusive work environment, the reconceptualization and restructuring of family–work balance, equal pay, parental leave, qualitative and affordable childcare, just to name a few—is facing us today again, under different circumstances, but with no less urgency. Why are these pressing issues yet to be addressed adequately? Even more disconcerting has been the rise of male violence against women, as the pandemic soars, a violence that often happens behind closed doors at the hands of partners and close family members. In short, despite the progress made, crises such as the COVID-19 pandemic reveal how fragile and volatile the presumed progress actually is. Is this progress real? Such a question arises spontaneously. If women still bear the greater burden of work associated with reproductive life, then it means that women—and men—are not done with their struggle.

Is this not what institutions of power are? The sedimentation of relations of domination into living spaces that leave little or no room for thinking or doing otherwise. Yet thinking and doing otherwise is the only way to regenerate possibilities, even when this appears to threaten its very foundations. Feminism, or women's movements, may be seen as threatening the foundations of existing power structures, but it may well be that new foundations are indeed needed.

In 1970 Carla Lonzi wrote:

> For a girl, the university is not the place where she will achieve her liberation by means of culture, but the place where, after having been carefully prepared by the family, her repression will be completed. Her education is a process of slow poisoning which paralyses her just as she is about to embark on more responsible gestures and enjoy experiences that will enlarge her conception of herself.[11]

Lonzi is speaking of the university as an institution of power that has been shaped and built on the premise of the exclusion of women as women. The question then becomes, how can that same institution transform itself from a place of exclusion and oppression to one where the young woman can affirm and express herself, "enlarge her conception of herself" without intimidation, without fear of being harassed or assaulted, without fear of being demoted, without fear of being silenced? And the same questions can be asked of other places, where she works, where she engages in politics, where she goes for entertainment, and even in her own home where she lives.

I began this introduction by saying that the impetus for this project came, in part, from the desire to reconnect with the experience of discovering feminism in and through my friendship with other female philosophy students—Laura, Gemma, Sara, Cristina—when studying at the University of Milan, in the late 1980s and early 1990s. It gives me pause to think that when I studied there, scarcely twenty years had passed since the early 1970s, when the women's movement exploded. Yet for as much as it did bring about change, where were the signs of women's revolt—the revolt within the revolt—in those buildings? How much had the university been changed by the women's movement in those twenty years? Some reforms following the 1968 student revolt had changed some key institutional rules but, as far as women were concerned, it was hard to say what actually had changed. At that particular time, when I discovered feminism, it felt as if it was starting then, at the moment when I happened to encounter it, oblivious to all that had already taken place. Perhaps, there is something to be said for "discovering" something through our own experience as if the world were actually opening up to us at that very moment, as if new. Unfortunately, the more common experience is that the world is felt as set in its ways, given as it is, closed. These women tell us clearly otherwise.

In these conversations, as I reflect on the words of Melandri, Muraro, and Cavarero and their invaluable work, the thread that connects different experiences of women at different moments becomes visible. In particular, their commitment to women's experience, and to the desire to name it, the friendship with women as a political practice, the ability to imagine a more just world, and the ability to listen to the recesses of our bodies, just to name a few, stand out as fruitful insights and concrete teachings. Carla Lonzi captures the message of their respective lifelong work fairly well, I think, and so it seems appropriate to close with her words:

> Our message to man, to the genius, to the rational visionary is this: the future of the world does not lie in moving continually forwards along a path mapped out by man's desire for overcoming difficulties. *The future of the world is open*: it lies in starting along the path from the beginning again with woman as a subject.[12]

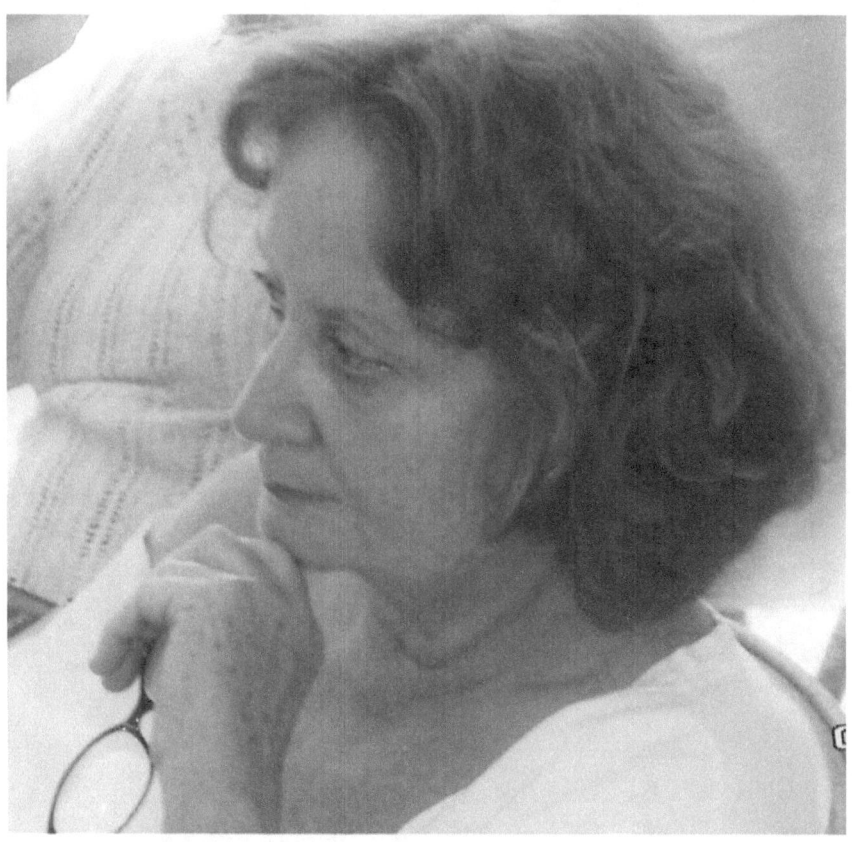

Lea Melandri. The author thanks Lea Melandri for the photo and kind permission to include it in this volume.

Lea Melandri was born in 1941 near Ravenna, Italy, in a small town named Fusignano, and has lived in Milan since 1967. She has taught in various schools and adult education courses. She currently offers courses at the Associazione per una Libera Università delle Donne in Milan (www.universitadelledonne.it), which she founded together with other women in 1987, and of which she is also the president. She participated in the women's movement in the 1970s. In 1971 she became the editor, together with the psychoanalyst Elvio Fachinelli, of the periodical *L'erba voglio* (1971–1978). She has also edited the anthology *L'erba voglio: Il desiderio dissidente* (Baldini & Castoldi 1998), which collects some of the articles of the periodical by the same name. Her ongoing writings and research center on the question of the sexes, which is reflected in her various publications: *L'infamia originaria* (Edizioni L'erba voglio 1977, Manifestolibri 1997, 2018); *Come nasce il sogno d'amore* (Rizzoli 1988, Bollati Boringhieri 2002); *Lo strabismo della memoria* (La Tartaruga edizioni 1991); *La mappa del cuore* (Rubbettino 1992); *Migliaia di foglietti* (Moby Dick 1996); *Una visceralità indicibile: La pratica dell'inconscio nel movimento delle donne degli anni Settanta* (Fondazione Badaracco, Franco Angeli 2000); *Le passioni del corpo: La vicenda dei sessi tra origine e storia* (Bollati Boringhieri 2001); *Preistorie: Di cronaca e d'altro* (Filema 2004); *Lettura a M. Fraire, R. Rossanda, La perdita* (Bollati Boringhieri 2008); *Alfabeto d'origine* (Neri Pozza 2017); *Amore e violenza: Il fattore molesto della civiltà* (Bollati Boringhieri 2011), translated into English as *Love and Violence: The Vexatious Factors of Civilization* (State University of New York Press 2019).

From 1987 to 1997, she directed the periodical *Lapis: Percorsi della riflessione femminile*, and, together with other women, she has edited the anthology *Lapis: Sezione aurea di una rivista* (Manifestolibri 1998). She has written various advice columns for several newspapers and has contributed to many newspapers, including: *Alfabeta, Internazionale, Il Manifesto, Il riformista*, and *Corriere della Sera* (http://www.enciclopediadelledonne.it/biografie/lea-melandri/). Between 2000 and 2004 she collaborated with the monthly publication *Carnet*. In 2012 she was awarded the Ambrogino d'oro as a "feminist theoretician." She is an honorary citizen of Carloforte, island of San Pietro.

One

The Memory of Our Body
(*La memoria del corpo*)

In Conversation with Lea Melandri

Elvira Roncalli In considering your life as a feminist from the end of the 1960s to this day, there is much to talk about. Perhaps you could start by telling us briefly about the most significant moments that have led you to do what you do and to be the woman you are.

Lea Melandri The immediacy with which, at the beginning of the 1970s, I joined feminism and the passion with which, to this day, I have kept giving continuity to its most original practices—such as *autocoscienza*[1] and the practice of the unconscious—show that mine is a choice with roots that go back to my childhood and to my family of origin. The experiences that are emotionally strong, both in suffering as in joy, leave a mark, wounds that are as deep as they are hidden. This is so much the case that they hardly become memories. I have called this "archive" of unspeakable experiences the "memory of our body" and I have sought to open a passageway (*varco*) to recover such experiences through the words of others. A sort of autobiography "through a third party." Even though I became aware of this and started to write about it rather late in life, the first twenty-five years of my life, which were spent in a peasant sharecropper family, very poor—three families crammed into a few rooms—counted as a particularly long and painful time. My parents gave me—their only daughter—the singular privilege of attending an excellent *liceo*[2] in the area. Yet, ever since my childhood, I shared the same bedroom with my parents, and I witnessed ways of being in a relationship in which it was impossible to distinguish between sexuality, quarrels, and violence. In my family, as in neighboring families, I saw women, working the land, working at home, looking after children, husbands, and brothers, women who were strong and vibrant but subjected to frail and tyrannical men, and who were mistreated and beaten. "Witnessing violence" (*violenza assistita*), they call it today. For me, it meant a great solitude. Thinking, studying, and love of learning and of the culture that was opening up before me were my "room of my own." It also meant a body that had been in some way violated, the loss of childhood and tenderness, even though my parents adored me and they never raised a hand to me. All these experiences contributed to a confused vision of women; they were caught between submission and the power of those who secured their material and emotional survival.

Another important moment destined, later on, to have an impact on my formation and my life choices was an experience that could have ended my educational journey early on. I had just arrived at school—about seven miles every day by bike—when I was given an essay to write on a seasonal theme, "November," which was something not unusual at the time. Instead of writing on this theme in a literary way, as I was expected, I wrote about the violence and the hardship that I had witnessed in my family. I was given my assignment back last, with a negative grade and just a note: "Very well written, but off topic [*fuori tema*]." All the most universal human experiences such as the social condition, sexuality, and family relations were "off topic"—but it took me years before I understood that. At the time, what I understood, even if only as a physical and psychological unease, was that a very painful part of my life did not enter school rooms and was not translatable into those learned languages (*linguaggi colti*). I stayed home for months and was only able to resume my studies because the teacher in question fell ill—by my good fortune—and a young woman poet came as a substitute. This was exactly what I needed.

You can imagine my happiness when, in 1968, after having just arrived in Milan, I encountered the non-authoritarian school movement (*movimento di scuola non autoritaria*) and almost at the same time, feminism, and for both of them the "off topic" was precisely the "topic." I entered the school system as a tenured teacher, and I could not only "dismiss" that role and what it had meant up to then but also approach my teaching according to what we used to call the "outrageous reversal" (*scandalosa inversione*) between life and culture. Life and personal experience moved to the center of the process of education, but also to the center of a political commitment capable of pushing itself to the roots of what is human.

ER You describe the experience in groups for a non-authoritarian school, which you joined in 1966, as a turning point in your life. You say the same of the women's movement and feminism. Please, speak about these two experiences: what they have been for you, how they intersect, and how they differ.

LM I arrived in Milan in November 1966, suddenly leaving behind two families—my family of origin and the one I had become part of through a marriage I did not want—and the *liceo* where I had just started teaching as a tenured teacher. I was twenty-five years old. Although I had contemplated it for some time, the flight happened as a sudden tear, when it seemed to me that my life had been defined once and for all: the *laurea* (university degree), marriage, a secure job. A horizon of dreams and expectations had just been eclipsed.

The train to Milan meant freedom, the flight from the ever-recurring identical time of the country, the possibility of a new birth. Only later did I discover that, at the end of the 1960s, many young people, men and women, had done the same thing. "The city makes one free" is a thought that has stuck with me always. Whenever I come back to Milan, after a trip, it is always as if I leave behind a little train station in the country.

The first year was not easy. Without a job, without a stable residence, I slept sometimes at the train station, on benches, as a guest of a couple from my same region, or at a budget hotel. But along with fears and anxieties, there was also the euphoria of a new beginning and the certainty that in such a large city nobody could find me and take me back. I have loved Milan for its streets, its trams, its bars, its phone booths, its parks. Anonymity made me feel protected.

The *turning point* that would change my life in a profound and lasting way came later, toward the end of 1968 when I was transferred as a teacher to a middle school in Melegnano[3] and I began to show interest in the teachers' meetings of the non-authoritarian school movement. Politics was finally coming closer to my most intimate needs. My most painful and significant experiences tied to the social condition, to being a woman, to sexuality, to family affections, all that had been left out, all that had been "off topic" in my entire educational journey, were becoming *the topic*. The choice to teach in the province and in a middle school was not accidental. I could meet students coming from rural areas who had been flunked several times in a school that had opened up to the masses and yet was very selective. By rejecting coercive and repressive means such as grades, disciplinary notes, and failures, I could help them speak, overcome passivity, fear, and yielding to the strongest.

In the spring of 1970, I met the psychoanalyst Elvio Fachinelli. I had read his interesting analyses of 1968, of youthful dissidence, of the need to bring the analytical interrogation outside the dual relationship between the analyst and the analyzed into places where major social changes were happening. These analyses are contained in *Il desiderio dissidente* (The dissident desire; February 1968), *Gruppo chiuso o gruppo aperto?* (A closed or an open group?; November 1968). Together with a group of organizers of a pedagogy course at the University of Milan, Fachinelli had just created a "self-managed preschool" (*autogestito*). He was preparing a conference on the non-authoritarian practices in schools, together with teachers, students, psychologists, and social workers.

My encounter with Milan's feminist groups happened the same year in which the periodical *L'erba voglio* began its publication, in 1971. The two paths are intertwined until 1975, when a conflict arose, both in my personal and intimate relationship with Elvio Fachinelli, and with the group of readers and collaborators of the periodical. They reproached us for the fact that the "separatism" of the feminist practice of *autocoscienza* was opening fractures in the editorial group.

I would say that, through feminism, the rediscovery of the relationship between the individual and the collective, the attention to the body and to the events that traverse it, were getting enriched with new awareness. First of which was the not so trivial fact that in the living singularity of the thinking body, there is inscribed the story of a different gender belonging (*appartenenza*).

ER Let's dwell a little more on your experience in the non-authoritarian school movement. Tell us a little more about the experience of the self-managed preschool.

LM The idea of creating a self-managed preschool was born, as I said, out of the pedagogy course at the University of Milan in the winter of 1968–1969 to which Elvio Fachinelli had been invited. It was supposed to be a "model institution of collective education," capable of taking into account the relations with the body and with the biological dimension of the individual. Behind this was the conviction that authoritarianism begins in childhood through the family and, in order not to raise passive and adapted individuals who are demotivated or violent, it is necessary to habituate children to a more natural and noncoercive self-regulation. Elvio Fachinelli had written that, starting in the family but also in preschools and in kindergartens, "whoever commands employs all the tools to forge fearful and law-abiding individuals, respectful of authority and of the established order, in such a way that they accept the destiny prepared for them: work and family, ordered escapes [*evasioni comandate*], and the vote every five years."[4] At the moment when the figure of the adult vested with authority and power is eliminated "one sees an iron hierarchy emerging, made of force and bullying; it is like finding oneself in a society that is between the fascist and the *mafioso*, and where the strongest protects those of his family." Fachinelli concluded by saying: "Here, the only politics that makes a minimum of liberatory sense is a radical politics, in the Marxian sense of the term, that is, one that takes human beings at their roots,"[5] from childhood.

At the beginning, placing oneself in a non-authoritarian situation was understood in a rigidly ideological way—not punishing, not stepping in when children get dirty or destroy what they are given—a freedom that was interpreted by some of the parents as weakness. After an initial experimental phase, it was understood that the relationship between the child and the adult entailed "a reciprocal learning, having fun and changing together."[6] It was as if we all had become, through that experience, kindergarten teachers.

ER Is it right, then, to understand "dissident desire," to use Elvio Fachinelli's expression, in the sense that it opposes a coercive authoritarian regime that constrains to obedience and passivity?

LM Yes, "dissident desire" means to leave behind the logic of dualism, the demolition of artificial and oppressive walls—for example, of the private to which woman has been relegated—but it also means to question notions and concepts presumably neutral and universals such as "man." It is a matter of leaving the "logic of the disastrous dialectic," as Elvio Fachinelli used to call it, which separates and opposes—nature-culture, body-mind, private-public, individual-society, and so forth—and of looking instead for the links (*nessi*) between what has been divided and opposed.

The book *L'erba voglio*,[7] which came out after the conference, collected writings by students, teachers, and others, precisely on the non-authoritarian practice in the schools. Through many voices, various and unusual communicative styles—the story of experiences by individual teachers, discussions of students, interviews, memos, disciplinary sanctions by principals—the main theme is the school as a "separate site," "formally without a relation to production" but, in fact, a tool that "a minority employs in order to reinforce and extend its privileges."[8] The school is shown as a site that institutionalizes relations of exploitation, hierarchies, roles, and differences enshrined by educational degrees, and a site that also organizes a consensus around an interpretation of reality removed from any criticism. Not unlike factories and society in general, there exists, in the school system, a minority that decides for the large numbers of students. For this reason, there is a centralized power on the one hand and a generalized subordination on the other. The non-authoritarian practice, according to its pioneer protagonists, does not propose an alternative culture, a new school, nor does it seek to democratize teaching methodologies. It is born as "an action of a negative type." It is the refusal of all rules to which the educational practice conforms itself—grades, exams, teacher's notifications, failures, schedules, programs. It is a practice that is both "destructive and liberating."

But the attack on the institution that, before anything else, acts as a "discipline of bodies," as regimentation and a training to obedience, as alienation of real knowledge from real life, as restraint of the creative capacities of the individual, is not without obstacles and psychological, social, and political difficulties. The "realized utopia," which the non-authoritarian school movement pursues, seeks ample and ambitious goals. Among them is a change in the conception and exercise of power, conceived as the separation between decision and execution, between a minority that controls society for its own ends and the masses that are excluded. Therefore, the matter is not a renewed school, or a "happy island," but a formative process that aims at leaving passivity and fear behind; it is about the presence and the participation of those who are excluded from power, the habit of assembly participation and of collective decision. In short, the matter is the exercise of power among equal and autonomous individuals. In the book, there are already the premises for the extension of non-authoritarian practices to other specific forms of oppression.

ER It is interesting that the experience of non-authoritarian practices goes to the roots of thinking and lands on the intuition—perhaps not new, but not easy to put into practice—that to change society's oppressive ways it is necessary to question all established relationships as they are and as they are lived. In other words, it is above all necessary to interrogate the relationship of domination and power, which is also what feminism does in those years, right?

LM What characterizes the feminism of the 1970s is the attempt to unearth a "dark" matter of experience that politics has always considered "other": body, sexuality, feelings, dreams, and in particular the relation of power between the sexes. It was the challenge to a form of politics, to institutions and languages that had been constituted in the absence of women. Women had been denied existence itself—as people, as individuals, they had been reduced to "gender." The choice of separatism on the part of feminism, a choice that was opposed by the "revolutionary" left of the extra-parliamentary groups,[9] meant the search for a profound *autonomy* from internalized models, from a vision of the world imposed by man and made one's own by women themselves, from the construction of a sociality among equals that had seen women only as "wives of," "mothers of." The analysis of man's domination shifted from the social scene, where it was seen only as a "feminine question," a disadvantage, and a discrimination, to a *personal story*. The body, sexuality, and motherhood became the first sites, the originary sites of the expropriation of existence, of the body, and of one's own creative capacities. The erasure of feminine sexuality, identified with procreation and therefore "naturalized," was seen as the origin of the confinement of women to the biological role of mother: submission and devotion to man, sacrifice of oneself. One did not speak of "freedom" but rather of "liberation," not of "difference" but of "differentiation," as the process that is at the bottom of all dualism.

ER The experience of the non-authoritarian school and the experience of feminism have in common a "destructive and liberating" practice. These two experiences came together for you in the 1970s. One can see this intersecting through the periodical *L'erba voglio* (1971–1977), which you created with Elvio Fachinelli. What were the specific reasons that led to the creation of this periodical? What were its aims?

LM Following the success of the book *L'erba voglio*, we decided to create a periodical by the same name with the idea of extending the non-authoritarian practices to other social spheres. Twenty-eight issues were published between 1971 and 1977 and a series of books were also published, as part of L'erba voglio Editions.

The goal of the periodical was to collect material from individuals and from groups in various cities, "to keep different voices together in a common range" (*tenere voci diverse in un insieme comune*), to stick to the logic of desire and of sharing in common (*accomunamento*), attracting the interest of, and involve, the "different social spheres" that characterized the students' dissidence of '68. From the very first issues, the editorial notes defined what would remain the key "lesson of *L'erba voglio*": "Authority and power are not topics discussed in the classroom. The pedagogical relation is not born on school desks. . . . Servitude and liberation today concern everyone or no one."[10]

The refusal to submit oneself to a singular language, of shutting oneself up in an organization is at the heart of the type of relation that the periodical established starting with readers who responded by sending back the card found in the book. The amount of material received was enormous just as surprising was the diversity and the multiplicity of voices, of ways of acting in context, and of the experiences attested to.

One could say that the periodical *L'erba voglio*, of which I was editor until 1976, and the women's movement that I encountered in 1971, were a prolongation of '68, its issues, and its radical political practices. Unfortunately, of that decade, we remember only the urban insurgency, terrorism, and the ebbing produced by armed fighting.

ER Your friendship and collaboration with Elvio Fachinelli was clearly important and fecund. There are probably many and various reasons for that. Would you share some?

LM The relationship with Elvio Fachinelli was both personal and political, an intimate relationship tightly intertwined with the activity of the periodical *L'erba voglio* until 1975. I had read his articles in *Quaderni Piacentini*[11] and I was struck by his ingenious interpretation of 1968 and of the changes happening in a mass society. Politics had been distant from me and it was Fachinelli's practice of bringing it closer to the "roots of the human," the interlacing of politics with psychoanalysis, that brought it close to me. In particular, what I would preserve and bring to my subsequent feminist analyses in the practices of *autocoscienza* and of the unconscious, is the definition of a "theoretical and practical field irreducible to the terms of the couple . . . the transition of the child from being a biological being to being inserted into a symbolic universe of man precisely."[12] Essentially, the reference to a "bio-psychological-sociological region" as the underlying thread of every topic that I would study later, and of my subsequent political practices.

If I talk almost exclusively of Elvio's thought, this is because his thought is what I saved, after having had "the courage to leave him"—as he said himself. The reasons that brought me to leave him and, a little later, to leave the periodical are intimate but also due to the fact that Elvio, even though he recognized the revolutionary scope of feminism, did not question himself in light of the challenges brought about by feminism regarding gender, sexuality, and sentimental relationships. He never understood why I would not preserve at least our friendship. I admit that I am a passionate person but I add that, when meeting him, I would criticize him again about his way of living his relationships with women. "You think over a woman's body," I had told him once, expecting that he would say, "Let's talk." Instead, silence. I understood that I had to resume my path on my own and with the women engaged with feminism. We met again, only once, in the mid-1980s. We had been asked to write a brief story of the journal *Lapis* for a collective book. I remember that we were both happy for the retrospective, and he said to me: "What a nice tandem we were, if only you had not left the periodical." Actually, I said, I had left him, and only reluctantly had I left the periodical, which I felt, was also, in part, my "creation." I cried at length, when I learned of his death, a few years later, in 1989. Two of our books, perhaps the most important ones, were published a year apart from each other. They are: *Come nasce il sogno d'amore*[13] and *La mente estatica*.[14] Since 1987, I directed the periodical *Lapis: Percorsi della riflessione femminile* (Lapis: Journeys of feminine reflection), which would be published for ten years with four hundred collaborators, in Italy and beyond. I definitely owe my passion for periodicals and journals to him, to the very intense years of *L'erba voglio*. He has been unjustly forgotten, and I am happy to have given him recognition and continuity in and through my long journey with feminism to this day.

ER The women's movement and feminism that caught on in the 1970s became your life. The experiences of those years have marked you profoundly and you keep returning to these experiences. One could almost go as far as saying that your theoretical elaboration is an ongoing revisitation of those years, events, and experiences. Do you agree with this characterization? Without intending to reduce the feminism of the 1970s to just a few moments, would you tell us which experiences are most significant and why?

LM   The interpretation of the women's movement of the 1970s has been a constant theme of my work. Even more: it has been an ongoing activity for me to see continuity or "resurgence" in the feminist waves that have increasingly occupied the squares and brought forth our struggles. The reason must be sought in the profound change that happened in that extraordinary season and from many points of view.

To discover the politics of lived personal experience, to get out of the dimension of the private and recognize each other in a collective history—which had been the history of men and women for centuries—to tell each other that history, in each other's presence, as women, to make it the object of reflection and to acquire conscious awareness (*presa di coscienza*) meant, for me, as for many other women, to be born to a new life. It created unprecedented relationships of friendship, love, and intelligence with other women, with our lives and with the world. We discovered a materiality of oppression that could not be reduced to economic exploitation, a specificity of domination that concerned us as women: the erasure of oneself as a person, as a singular individual, the reduction to a role—"wife of," "mother of"—and to a gender, a homogeneous whole, a sexuality at the service of others, motherhood as the obligation to procreation. The challenge of feminism could not be more ambitious: "starting from oneself" was seen as the necessary passage "to alter the world," and sexism as the foundational act of politics, now shaken in its foundation.

What moved me passionately then—and honestly, what moves me still now—was an analysis of the personal experience pushed to its extreme regions, situated between the unconscious and consciousness, the excavation into the memory of our body. Reappropriation of the body meant recognizing and legitimizing one's own sexuality but also removing the question of health from the invasion of medical science. Having a voice of one's own (*presa di parola*)—thus the birth into the polis—happened through this tenacious and proclaimed adherence to the body, to the internal world, as a rediscovery of the lasting signs that man's history has left on it, therefore "political" in themselves.

Together with Lia Cigarini and other feminist women, we authored the document "Pratica dell'inconscio e movimento delle donne" (Practice of the unconscious and the women's movement), published in the periodical *L'erba voglio* in 1974. This was the premise that led to the birth of two groups in Milan, the "analysis group" and the "practice of the unconscious group," which were later created in Rome as well. At the time, I was also the editor of the periodical *L'erba voglio* and many of my articles were published there, but I was also trying to push for a confrontation, a wrestling (*un corpo a corpo*), with theories that did not anticipate, in their idea of revolution, the presence on the political scene of that "unforeseen subject"—"soggetto imprevisto"—as Carla Lonzi called it, that women were and of the "new savages"—"nuovi selvaggi"—in the words of Elvio Fachinelli, that students were. If I return persistently to those years, it is because the radical demands that emerged then, as a "possible" in that "impossible" moment, are destined to re-present themselves again. This is the idea inscribed in the slogan "change yourself and change the world," the search for the links (*nessi*) between sexuality and economy, between sexuality and politics, sexuality and the symbolic.

ER Was the women's movement of the 1970s a mass movement? Was it a homogeneous movement? Who were the women who participated in it? Were they, for the most part, young? Students? What brought women out to protest in the open squares?

LM I cannot quantify in terms of numbers and thus I am not able to say if it was a mass movement. The great demonstrations in the squares and the fashion of flowery skirts made it seem like a mass movement, especially with the rapid spread of the practice of *autocoscienza* in the most unthinkable places, from factories to newspapers' newsrooms, to the trade unions' headquarters, and above all, the attention of the media, including television. Never have women, speaking about themselves, appeared more threatening to the roles, to the identities of both sexes, which had been considered "natural" for centuries of one and the other sex. Rai Uno (one of the main public TV stations), for about two years, between the end of the 1970s and the beginning of the 1980s, broadcast documentaries and interviews by feminists. On Radio Tre (one of the main public radio stations), Rossana Rossanda directed a program called *The Other Women*, where she interviewed the most committed feminist women on key words of politics. To speak of masses and of homogeneity would mean not taking into account the fact that it was a movement that was always characterized—even after the 1970s—by a plurality of voices, theories, and practices that, in turn, could assume more relevance than others, but never erase them. The confrontation, the possibility of contrasting one another in the story that one gave of oneself, in the words that one employed was felt as a strength, as a push for change. I am convinced that even the "double militance"—women who were part of feminist groups, but also of extra-parliamentary groups such as Lotta Continua, *Il Manifesto*, Avanguardia Operaia, and Potere Operaio—contributed to maintain a vital tension between the specificity of our analyses and practices and the broader horizon of social struggles against the capitalist system.

We can say without hesitation that it was an intergenerational phenomenon, made of young and not so young people who rebelled against tradition, families, parties, and the institutions marked by patriarchy, against real or symbolic mothers; people who believed they could attack and upend an economic and political system that wanted them integrated, alienated, and happy. As Fachinelli intuited, these subjects were not to be viewed in terms of class or according to the logic of needs. Rather, they were "fluid like crystals" and spread without any need for Bibles, moved by the logic of "desire" and "freedom," and therefore also outside the logic of a setback. They would "recrystallize" in other times and in other places. And they did. Today, there are very young girls and boys who still read with curiosity the periodical *L'erba voglio* and invite me to talk about the non-authoritarian movements of the 1970s.

ER How would you describe masculine domination? What forms and structures does it have? How has it changed, if it has changed in these last fifty years?

LM If we want to see change in the relationship between the sexes as we have inherited it, we must recognize that it is a particular kind of domination, different from all others, simply because it is intertwined and confused with the most intimate experiences, such as sexuality and motherhood. This is not all, though. Confined outside history and restricted to a submissive but not, for that reason, less important role, such as the care and raising of children, women have forcibly made man's vision of the world their own. The victim speaks the same language as the perpetrator. What else could they have done to survive, if not wedging themselves in the functions that were imposed on them, in order to receive some pleasure and some power?

It is the consciousness of this "invisible violence"—both cultural and symbolic—that marked the beginning of the feminism of the 1970s. It differs from the emancipation struggles that preceded it and that continue to exist next to a women's movement to this day that still speaks of "liberation" from internalized models. The crisis of patriarchy was already evident fifty years ago. Yet within a domination that—as Pierre Bourdieu says in *Masculine Domination*[15]—is inscribed in institutions, and in the shadow of bodies, where permanencies are stronger than changes. What we have been able to observe, and painfully so, is that when faced with women's greater freedom and with some timid signal of masculine consciousness, sexism is back in its most archaic and savage forms, as a power of life and death with an alarming sequence of rapes and femicides. Today, we speak of that. We finally say that we are confronted with a structural phenomenon. But then the tendency persists to present this violence as crime news, as an individual's pathology or the result of backward cultures. Again, compared with the past, there is today a global feminist network, Non Una Di Meno,[16] that has placed violence against women at the center of its political practice, which besides the big mobilization of women in Argentina in 2016 has also seen the first demonstration in Italy of the "lesbian and feminist collectives" in 2007, with banners that stated: "The killer has the house keys." Even if slowly, we have succeeded in opening the house doors and looking inside families and couple relationships, which, until not long ago, were still protected by the rhetoric of the family and not only that.

ER Violence against women, femicide, thus persists, despite the fact that relationships among the sexes have changed. In your book *Love and Violence: The Vexatious Factors of Civilization* (*Amore e violenza: Il fattore molesto della civiltà*), recently translated and published in English,[17] you claim that there is an unsuspected connection (*legame*) between kinship and violence and that it is necessary to excavate the "love dream" in order to arrive at the roots of this violence. Would you explain this relation between love and violence? If love and violence are so tied, to uproot such a violence would require rethinking our way of conceiving and living love. How do we do that?

LM It has definitely been a big step forward to recognize that male violence against women cannot be read only in terms of criminality or pathology of the individual, and that instead it must be placed inside the culture that we have inherited, which is marked by the domination of one sex over the other. There remains, above all among men, a resistance to recognize themselves as a "gender," to say that the violence by some concerns them all, insofar as it is inscribed in what is considered "normality." Therefore, a resistance to analyze violence even in its least visible and most elusive aspects. There are many women who do not denounce violence, many people who do not consider it a crime, victims who return to live with the one who has tried to kill them. For preventative measures to be effective, it is important therefore that violence be not isolated in its manifest forms—

rapes, abuses, homicides—not isolated from the culture where it happens, and presented in all its ambiguity in the institutions and in manners of feeling and thinking of both men and women.

Some questions need to be raised. How does it happen that a violence that has been present for centuries in the relationship between man and woman has become an "emergency" in Italy, only in the last few years? One could say, only since the publication of the first National Reports[18] on the alarming causes of women's death. How is it that women themselves who suffer this violence daily hesitate to bring it out, expose it, and denounce it? Is it only because of fear? Or is it because it is difficult to recognize it, and distinguish it from love? Regardless of the many attempts of shifting the figure of the aggressor onto someone unknown or onto backward cultures, daily news and statistics say that it is husbands, brothers, lovers, and men who are sentimentally tied to the victims who rape, kill, and persecute women. This means that we are faced with a very particular kind of violence, which has an unsuspected and a perverted kinship with love. *One does not kill for love, but love matters*. My book speaks precisely about this "unsuspected" and perverse relation. Masculine domination that after having been "naturalized" for centuries has been brought back to its historical context is, above all, the domination that has been confused with the most intimate relationships, with sexuality and motherhood. Before being a father and an authoritarian and violent husband, man is a tender child. The ambiguity is evident. Man rages against the body that has engendered him, that has cared for him first, that has given him the first sexual solicitations. This is the body that he finds again in his adult love life, and through which he dreams of reliving the originary intimate belonging, the unity of two at birth. But it is also the body that has kept him in its clutches (*in balia*) at the moment of his great dependence and helplessness, a body that could give him life or death, care or neglect. By confining woman to the role of mother, man has constrained himself to remain a child too, to wear a mask of virility always under threat.

Masculine dominance has never failed. But for a century now many great changes have occurred. It is within the domestic sphere that women have shown that they don't want to be a body at others' disposal. As long as women have continued to take upon themselves the care of the children, of the elderly, and of the sick, and make the life of their husbands, sons, and brothers good and perfectly healthy, men could think of themselves as "free" from biological ties and from everything that implied "being a body," with its fragilities, dependencies, and needs. In some way, this was a privilege; in other ways, it was a mutilation of essential aspects of the human, such as the hardship and the joy of caring for the growth of a child. If the male community that governs the world keeps causing death with such facility, perhaps it is precisely because man has lacked this familiarity with bodies and with life as a whole.

ER Is this why you call the violence against women "invisible"? A violence that is so ingrained in the fabric of society and culture that it is hard to see, but also in the sense that one does not look hard enough to see it. Is it so? How to explain this blindness?

LM The expression "invisible violence" appears in one of my first articles in the 1970s and the reference, at the time, was to a vision of the world, to a way of thinking and a feeling of oneself that women had unknowingly made their own, even though it had been produced by the only sex that had a voice in history. But sexism is "invisible," and slow to become a conscious awareness, also because of a culture that has "privatized" it and "naturalized" it. For centuries and, under many respects still today, the submission of women has been the "normality." When I returned to this issue, at the beginning of the year 2000, in coincidence with the appearance of the alarming National and International Reports on women's first cause of death,[19] I had to ask myself why even I, who for years had witnessed the violence against women in my family, had become aware of it so late. I could say the same of Italian feminism, despite the anti-violence centers that have existed since the 1980s. The answer that I have given is that love as we have inherited it, with its obligations, its dependencies, its illusions of intimate belonging to another being, has been able to serve as a veil over the violence and the power relations that are tied to it. If violence in such obvious forms as abuses, rapes, and femicides is so elusive, we can say that it is precisely the love dream, as a dream of unity between two, that prevents us from recognizing it as such.

ER Besides your experience in the non-authoritarian school movement and in the women's movement, there is another significant experience to which you return often and that is your teaching for the "150-hour courses." For those who are not familiar with the "150-hour school," could you explain what it was? Who participated in it?

LM When I applied to be transferred from the middle school of Melegnano to the "150-hour courses"[20]—a great conquest of the working-class struggles for those who had not received the middle school diploma—I was fully in the midst of my feminist involvement. I was deeply convinced that the man–woman relation was the central question for rethinking politics, its institutions, but also it entailed history, culture, and disciplinary knowledges and languages. I was committed to bringing into my role as a teacher the new awareness coming from the women's movement. I knew that, in the "150-hour courses," I would find less bureaucracy and less constraints regarding the programs so it would be easier to introduce into my lesson plans the themes close to my heart, which had always been left outside school. Although I knew that it was a predominantly working-class school, the desire was to find women's presence. I was assigned to a school very late, in early December 1976, and I arrived at the school on via Gabbro 6, in Affori-Bovisasca,[21] without too many expectations. I was greatly surprised when, on entering the classroom, I found about thirty women and a few men. The emotion was such that I sat down in the first open chair I found, and the woman next to me—thinking I was also a student—reassured me by saying that there had been a substitute and that "we had not done anything yet." It was a new turning point, and it would mark my life, my interests, and my choices to this day.

The thirty, no longer young "students," were all housewives and they had had to work hard to get a "school section" to open in their area. The trade unionists, fixated on the idea of a school for the working class, could not understand why women who had been, until then, wives and mothers, dedicated to the care of the family, wanted to go back to school and obtain a middle school diploma that they would probably never have a use for. As soon as we started discussing themes that made those women more aware of what their life had been up to that moment, it was as if a door had opened and, once gone through—as one of them said—it was no longer possible to go back. The happiness of the discoveries they were making was immediately expressed with posters, flyers, handouts that they would prepare with the mimeograph, and whose titles revealed the change that had happened within them and that would affect other women in other areas of Milan. I remember some: *Più polvere in casa meno polvere nel cervello* (More dust in the house, less dust in the brain)—in the picture of the poster, a little woman was dusting her head—*L'uovo terremotato* (The shaken egg)—a big cracked egg out of which lines of women flow—*È sparita la donna pallida e tutta casalinga* (The pale and all-around housewife woman has disappeared), *Acrobate* (Acrobat women), *La traversata* (The crossing).

For the women who took the course (*le corsiste*) it was the rediscovery of a life spent inside the family in light of a new awareness. Their writings, born spontaneously under the impetus of the desire to tell each other things with a freedom they had not known until then, were in no way rhetorical or scholastic. They went straight to the truth that surfaced gradually through thinking and discussing with other women. For me, it was again like finding figures of my past, women that resembled those in my family, in my small town. It was like mending, in some way, the tear that had occurred between us through my studies and finally finding a shared language with which to speak to one another and reflect on our various experiences. I remember, in particular, Amalia Molinelli, a peasant woman from the Emilia region, who had migrated with her family to the city. She had had the hardest jobs and had cultivated in silence and in solitude profound thoughts that found immediate expression in her writing. It was a very creative language, a mix of dialect and Italian that entered, without intimidation, specialized subjects—mathematics, philosophy, physics—messing them up, forcing them to confront personal life, the everyday, the different destiny that had befallen the male and the female. Years later, a book was published with the title *I pensieri vagabondi di Amalia* (The vagabond thoughts of Amalia).

ER I am struck by how this experience deals with themes and issues you have already explored through the non-authoritarian school movement and feminism, showing again the relation between knowledge, institutions, and power. For how long has this experience lasted and what has it meant for you?

LM Ever since 1976, the course in Via Gabbro had become exemplary and the women who attended it were like "pioneers," showing the potential that school and education have in altering the traditional roles of women. The Affori experience drew immediate attention from newspapers and television, so much so that, with a friend who was also a film director, we thought of letting people know about it in a creative way. The documentary movie by Adriana Monti, *Scuola senza fine* (School without end), tells the story of some of the women in the course and their encounter with me, and it was shown at New York University, in December 1984, as part of a conference on Italian and American Directions: Women's Film Theory and Practice. Unfortunately, the two books that present this experience and that became better known abroad than in Italy are no longer available.[22]

Once they finished the course that gave them the middle school diploma, in June 1976, as expected, the women who had attended the course with such an enthusiasm no longer wanted to go back home. Therefore,

I had to invent "monograph courses"—initially without any institutional recognition—"experimental two-year courses," and we used the rooms that the school made available to us. I invited feminist friends, who had knowledge and practices to share, to teach courses, to give lessons, and to work in groups. The majority of these women guests came from the group born in 1977 in Col di Lana[23] called "sexuality and writing." In 1980, thanks to a European fund, the Cooperativa Gervasia Broxon was born in a one-room place in Bovisasca. The name was invented but nobody asked who Gervasia Broxon was. The participants were the same as the first 1976 course plus others who had gradually joined. The aim of the cooperative was to prepare them to become graphic designers but, behind this, was the idea of questioning disciplinary knowledge and work in light of a culture that had excluded women, by considering them "natural" custodians of the family. Equally important was the analysis of the relationships that were established among us, teachers and students, and the opportunity to rethink our educational formation in light of the life experiences that had remained outside it.

In Affori-Bovisasca I spent the most intense ten years of my teaching and of my feminist commitment—between 1976 and 1986, when the cooperative closed. Even though I did not live in that neighborhood, I spent the greatest part of my life there, as if I were literally giving shape to another "town" similar to the one I had left behind in Romagna. I also think of the joy of sharing the passion for *ballo liscio* (ballroom dancing) with my students, men and women. In the basement of the place, every occasion was good to celebrate with a party and a dance.

ER Without any doubt an extraordinary experience that made its way to the United States with a movie and a book! It shows the radicality of an initiative that creates spaces where women can give words to their experience and how earth-shaking this is. There is an image that you provide speaking about this experience, where the *corsiste*—the women who took the course—to whom the concept of a unit of measure had been explained in the abstract "invented thousands of counterexamples for measuring the perimeter of the room, by taking their hands, stretching and squeezing with pleasure . . . their body was the unit of measure/yardstick of space" (*inventavano mille controesempi sulla possibilità di misurare il perimetro della stanza prendendosi per mano, allungandosi o stringendosi a piacere . . . il loro corpo era l'unità di misura dello spazio*).[24] This idea of one's own body as a measuring unit is really powerful; it seems to provide the basic formula for women's politics, something that you say "you continue to think of, excitedly," and you add: "a political practice that goes through the body without letting itself be swallowed up by the body." Please, tell us more about the body as a measuring unit and about this politics of the body.

LM To name the radicality of the practices of the feminism of the 1970s, I have often used the expression "matters of the body" (*problematiche del corpo*), meaning by this all the lived experiences and passions having the body at their center: sexuality, motherhood, abortion, and so on. The separation of the body from the polis appeared in all its magnitude for the first time; the exclusion of women from the public sphere, but also the exclusion of all those spheres of the human—and even the most universal ones—that have been identified as feminine: birth, death, love, feelings, emotions, dreams. To place the body at the center has meant to bring to awareness the materiality of the expropriation that women have suffered: erasure of their sexuality, motherhood as destiny, procreative obligation. The reappropriation started there, from a body with which they had been identified and to which others had given names, forms, and fictions. It also meant to rediscover the unconscious rooting of sexism in the memory of the women's bodies themselves. After those revolutionary beginnings, in comparison to what had been seen only as a "feminine question"—a disadvantage to be made up, an imperfect citizenship—feminism risked moving toward kinds of theorizing that were more elaborate but also more distant from personal experience. The encounter with the women in my "150-hour course" was, for me and for many feminist friends, the happy occasion to return to a greater concreteness. It provided the opportunity to interrogate our intellectual formation, the languages we employed, and to understand how much of our lives had remained untranslated and untranslatable into those specialized subjects and into those languages. The idea of being able to measure the perimeter of the room with their bodies was less odd than it might seem at first. With their bodies as wives and mothers, those women had measured the rooms of their houses; in those bodies, they had buried feelings and thoughts that could not be presented to their very families. It is not by accident that, when the door for expressing them was opened, writings of incredible lucidity and depth regarding the woman condition were produced.

ER In some of your writings, you differentiate between "word" and "writing." You describe "word" as a means that can lead to one's own discovery, but the word remains more fleeting and tenuous, whereas you describe "writing" as a more "solid ground." You also write that these observations find their origin in the practice of the unconscious and of *autocoscienza*, which are feminist practices of the 1970s, and from this you come to "experiential writing." Tell us more about the practice of the unconscious and of *autocoscienza*, and why they were so important. How are they tied to what you call "experiential writing"?

LM   I don't know when I started using the expression "experiential writing" (*scrittura di esperienza*)[25] and, because I don't like definitions, I have not worried about giving it a more precise outline. It is as if it imposed itself by itself, without my knowing, and came back to me as a competence, as a particular way of understanding culture outside known styles—literature, essays, and so forth—even outside the style that resembles it the most, namely, autobiography. Hence, I have to take a step back and ask myself: Where did this interest originate in me? Through which paths did it manifest itself? How to characterize it? My first example of "experiential writing" (*scrittura di esperienza*) is the one I have already mentioned: the essay "November," which I wrote while a student in high school and which became the occasion for writing about my peasant family working the land, the misery and the difficult relationships with my parents, the solitude and the feeling of guilt for being the only daughter and able to study.

Many years later, in 1968, in Milan, as I have already said, I found a sort of compensation through the non-authoritarian practices in schools, when Elvio Fachinelli asked me to write about my experience in the Melegnano middle school. My piece was titled "Due anni di esperienza non autoritaria nella scuola media di Melegnano" (Two years of non-authoritarian experience in the middle school in Melegnano) and was included in the book *L'erba voglio*.[26] The "off topic"—subjectivity, lived experience, everything that is closed within the private and is thought to be unsayable except in literary fiction—became "the topic," legitimized by a movement that thought of politics as a process capable of taking the human "at its roots" and favored "a totality of manifestations of human life." Feminism will pick up the subjective experience again in its most archaic sediment, that of the "first root" of human relationships, which is sexual differentiation.

The word spoken within the small feminist groups of *autocoscienza*, of collectives, of conferences, of assemblies, became the fulcrum of self-narration and self-reflection. It helped in abandoning a certain order of sense and identifying other meanings. It allowed the birth of the dream, its unveiling, doing and undoing one's own story through the gaze of other women. It is therefore possible to relive the roles of the masculine and the feminine—as an abstract opposition of emotions and reason—while having, at the same time, the possibility of analyzing them by keeping some distance from them.

Attention to the written word and the idea that writing could be an important transition in the construction of feminine individualities, released from models and conditionings, emerged, as far as I am concerned, in the mid-1970s, in correspondence with the beginning of my teaching the "150-hour course," a course taken almost entirely by women. The group "sexuality and writing," which I had created with other feminists in order to not lose the originality of those practices, would continue side by side, intersecting with the courses offered to women: courses as part of compulsory education, monograph courses, the experimental two-year courses, the courses of the Broxon cooperative, and, finally, courses of the Free University of Women (Libera Università delle Donne) in Milan, in 1987. In other words, the same women would move from one context to the other. It was this experience that made me understand that, in contrast with one's own biography, and with one's own experience, narration changes once it comes out of solitude, out of the private, out of the secret of a drawer in order to be exposed to the presence and the listening of others. And I understood, vice versa, how much the so-called objective, technical, specialized writing changes when it is questioned in light of its relation to autobiography and to the imaginary that supports it.

ER In light of what you just said, it seems that the "experiential writing" (*scrittura di esperienza*) is the writing of the body, a writing that digs into one's own depths, into the sedimentations that have built up at the bottom of our being and that are at the border between the conscious and the unconscious. You call it a "border region," which arrives at the "entrails of history," at "prehistory." Unlike autobiography, which composes a homogeneous whole, this kind of writing decomposes and undoes. Why is this experiential writing so vital? Autobiography leads to a sense of continuity and unity; but a movement that goes back and forth, such as that of experiential writing, where does it lead?

LM In the early 1980s, my field of observation broadened and, for certain aspects, deepened in coincidence with a long personal analysis. I was surprised by an unusual type of writing, made of short sentences, fragments marked by a fantastic undertone, emotional and tied to personal experiences. My discovery of Sibilla Aleramo, the advice column (*posta del cuore*), private writings in *Ragazza in* and in *Noi Donne* belong to this very period.[27]

In another way, however, the object of my writing seems to narrow down to just one theme: the love dream, its "permanence," which is almost timeless in human relationships. This is the time when the kinship between writings considered scrap writings (*di scarto*)—letters, diaries, writings kept in the drawer—and specialized writings, between the sentimentalism attributed to women and one of the most lasting myths of masculine thought, that is, the androgynous ideal—the "creative mind" of which Virginia Woolf writes in *A Room of One's Own*—became more evident.

In this period, I rediscovered Sibilla Aleramo, not as a poet but as a "forerunner" of feminine consciousness. Aleramo defines her work as "a fury of unceasing self-creation," an "enormous sum of life." In her *Diario* (Diaries),[28] once she abandons autobiography as the construction of an ideal image of herself, that "narrating self" becomes a sort of self-analysis, a continuous unveiling: "veils all to be lifted." The search for the autonomy of the feminine being hits against "a representation of the world that has been aprioristically admitted and later understood thanks to analysis," Sibilla lucidly intuits. While she writes her *Diaries*, Sibilla realizes that she is losing her poetic inspiration and that there is, in her, a "subterranean second life, a tacit current of thoughts and feelings" that she cannot translate into poetry, except by "doing violence to myself, making myself inhuman, perhaps even killing myself." For this other dimension, another writing was necessary, the same as that of her daily notes, and for which she was reproached as "chatting on paper." It is a type of writing capable of going very close to life, of retracing its own steps, an ongoing back and forth between ruptures and awakenings of consciousness.

Through this kind of writing, Aleramo comes to the awareness of being a woman and anticipates what the 1970s feminism will bring to light, namely the vision of a masculine world that women have internalized. The awareness of Sibilla is, from this point of view, the most precious and controversial inheritance that she hands down to the generations that come after her. She writes: "I have had to adapt my intelligence to yours, with an effort of decades: to understand man, to learn his language, has meant distancing from myself. Actually, I do not express myself, I do not translate myself either: I reflect your representation of the world, aprioristically admitted, then understood by way of analysis . . . this clash [*cozzo*] between my internal rhythm and the rhythm of the forms that you have found! How to free myself? It would be necessary that you listen to me as if I were dreaming."

I find it important to say that all these writings—Aleramo, Michelstaedter, Nietzsche, and the advice column (*posta del cuore*)—that appear in my book *Come nasce il sogno d'amore* are not treated as material to be studied, nor have I thought of creating a genre. I have approached them with a procedure that I would call *rewriting*: trail the text, trace it, let myself be seduced, fuse and confuse myself with it, and then deviate from it just enough to show, extoll, and discover what is not said. Again, dream and lucidity in an entanglement that is difficult to disentangle, a self-analysis done through other alter egos, voices, faces, and metaphors that are carried inside, in that primordial landscape that is the "memory of our body," always ready to sink in the mystery and the unsayable.

ER It seems as if you are referring to a materiality that is at the origin of everything, a materiality that goes through women's body but that does not go through history. If it is so, how can we let it emerge?

LM The feminism of the 1970s has the merit of having brought to light the awareness of the "materiality" of oppression and exploitation that did not coincide with historical materialism. In one of the early articles, "L'infamia originaria" (The originary infamy),[29] published in the periodical *L'erba voglio*, I wrote about "economic survival" and distinguished it from "emotional survival." To those who sought to take every form of domination and bring it back to economic exploitation, I would point out the difference between the commodification of the worker's body and the destiny allotted to the feminine sex to embody the "first" commodity, the commodity par excellence. The worker is a laboring force that, by selling himself to the employer, makes of his body a commodity, without however losing his individuality, which affirms itself inside his family in a position turned upside down as a patriarch in relation to his wife and children. The woman, as already said, has been identified with the body, a body to which others have given shape, names, and fiction. The worker makes himself a commodity, but the woman is an exchange commodity among men. Just as in economic exploitation, something is "repressed" that needs to be brought back to history, but its roots go deep to a very particular domination, which is intertwined and confused with the most intimate experiences, those of motherhood and sexuality. This is why this "repression" encounters obstacles when one tries to bring it to awareness. If sexism persists, so elusive that even to this day it is still not seen as a structural phenomenon, it is also because women themselves, forcibly, have made it their own, and they have become one of the transmission links in their own enslavement. It is no accident that the "invisible violence," or "symbolic violence," is at the heart of the analyses and practices of feminism before manifest violence such as rapes, femicides, abuses, and so on.

ER The practice of *autocoscienza* keeps coming back as a foundational and fundamental experience of your being as a woman. If the practice of *autocoscienza* has been so important, why has it been abandoned? Has it been abandoned? Where to find it today, if it is still practiced?

LM With *autocoscienza*, the process of knowing moved in the proximity of the body, of the memory that has been deposited there. *Autocoscienza* opposed political generalization with the practice of "starting with oneself." Carla Lonzi wrote, "The blockage has to be forced by each woman one by one, a necessary step for the birth of one's own individuality" (*Il blocco— scrisse Carla Lonzi—va forzato una per una, passaggio necessario per la nascita della propria individualità*).[30]

This process where the individual woman could "move closely to the lived experiences of everyone" also needed the physical presence of other women, of relationships among women, *outside* the male gaze—and this is what separatism allowed. The knowledge of *autocoscienza* could not substitute the transformation that happens while practicing it. Feminine subjectivity is born in this particular relationship among individuals who are similar (*tra simili*), and, in this sense, *autocoscienza* is not the practice of a particular historical time, it is "not finished." Together with its theoretical scope, it is the form that the feminine discourse on the body and on sexuality has taken and that could not avoid a reckoning with psychoanalysis. Its permanence has to be put in relation with the fact that sexuality does not belong to this or that particular epoch; it is not just a component of personal life but a supporting structure of society in all its aspects. I agree with Manuela Fraire, a feminist psychoanalyst who has written that *autocoscienza* "was abandoned precociously as a tool," and that its outcomes have been collected, in part, by certain writings that still preserve its traces.[31]

Difficulties and obstacles began to emerge when feminism expanded outside the small groups of *autocoscienza*, the urban collectives, to enter institutional environments of culture and politics, when we went from the "feminist movement" to a "diffused feminism" (*femminismo diffuso*). Even though the expansion was desirable, the risks that this entailed were immediately evident: "A massive operation of expropriation and redefinition of the knowledge produced by women on the part of political and cultural institutional environments" (*Un'operazione massiccia di esproprio e ridefinizione del patrimonio prodotto dalle donne, da parte di ambiti istituzionali della politica e della cultura*).[32]

Two directions imposed themselves. One sought to safeguard "spaces of self-governance and autonomy inside the university"; the other sought to establish a strong subject, a women's "tradition" that, as such, needed an "authority" and a "language" of a symbolic order upon which to ground itself.

The periodical *Lapis* represented an alternative path, critical of both the thought of sexual difference and of the proliferation of "gender studies" in academia. *Lapis*'s editorial staff sought to provide continuity and development of the practice out of which feminism was born: the search for links (*nessi*) between politics and life, between self-knowledge and the "one hundred orders of language" with which we are also imbued; an *autocoscienza* that is able to question the knowledge and the powers of public life; "a geography, not a genealogy," a knowledge that is not afraid to delve into "polluted landscapes," to plumb the relationship between man and woman in all its complexity and contradictions.

I have sought to give continuity to *autocoscienza* and to the practice of the unconscious through my "workshops on experiential writing," to stay close to what has been deposited in the memory of our body and that resists even in becoming a memory. The throughway (*tramite*) represented by the fragments of writing of other women and other men legitimizes, in some way, the exposure of oneself that today finds its obstacle in the gossip on television and on social media, where lived experience has gone back to being "private" again.

Through the practice of *autocoscienza*—telling each other and reflecting on one's own experience together with other women—personal lives took on a relevance they never had before. They became the place of an unwritten story to be rediscovered in its entirety; in particular, the story of the relationship between the sexes, a domination that was confused with intimate life and that could be brought to awareness only by starting precisely there. And could be modified as well. This double move (*doppio movimento*)—turning one's gaze to oneself and, at the same time, turning oneself to listen to, turning one's attention to the experience of other women—seems to be lost, together with the practices that are able to keep together *individual and collective, body and thought*. Feminism itself, spreading into the traditional places of knowledge, into public institutions, moved away more and more from the radical approach of its beginnings, which was to question life in its entirety. With the social network, one gets used "to looking at oneself outside" (*guardarsi fuori*)—not *from* the outside—

through a self-representation that seems to close itself up. The impression is an amalgamation where it is no longer possible to distinguish between outside and inside. The risk is not only that of no longer being able to tell one's experience, but also of not being able to experience in the first place.

ER You have just made reference to the thought of sexual difference as one of the directions that has affirmed itself in Italy and that has become well known both inside and outside Italy. You have been critical of the thought of sexual difference, in particular with regard to the symbolic figure of the mother as a source of feminine authority and legitimation. Would you talk about the most salient points of your critique of the thought of sexual difference?

LM When I considered motherhood and its enduring appearance in the women's movement, the first question I raised was whether we have to consider it a "permanence," something that does not change, a role that we inherit from what has traditionally been considered the "feminine difference"—a difference deduced, more or less conceptually, from the biological capacity of having children—or whether it is it a factor of change, as one part of feminism, tied to the Milan Women's Bookstore, seemed to consider it. How is it possible that precisely what had been the reason for excluding women from public life—reducing them to something completely homogeneous such as a gender, the identification through sex, the body, sexuality, and the necessary care for life's preservation—could become, with a simple *reversal* (*capovolgimento*) from negative to positive, an opportunity for emancipation, for liberation or for feminine power?

I deliberately employ the word *emancipation* to refer to the emancipation between the 1800s and 1900s, and also to the philosophical theories of the thought of sexual difference of the 1980s and 1990s, as well as to what today is called the "feminization" of the public space, which even some feminist groups view as an opportunity to acquire power and bring significant changes to the workplace and politics. I reserve, on the contrary, the word *liberation* to the discrepancy, or discontinuity (*scarto*), that has produced, in the historic consciousness, the feminism of the 1970s, in which the identification of woman with mother, of sexuality with procreation, were precisely the object of critique and change. We essentially realized that the most profound expropriation that women have suffered, even more than their role in procreating, concerns their individuality, their being persons ahead of being wives and mothers. It is only at the moment when women recognize and legitimize their own sexuality that motherhood can become a choice.

The theme of "sexual difference" identified once again with the figure of the mother redefined as a positivity can be interpreted—at least for the Italian feminism at the end of the 1970s—as a return to more reassuring positions, as an exit from practices that seemed to distance women even more from the polis, having pushed politics to the borders of the unconscious. These practices seemed as endless as Penelope's shroud.

According to the thought of sexual difference, the greatness and the superiority of the mother do not depend on her biological capacity of procreating, but on the fact that she is the one who gives body and word. This is the originary superiority that has to be recognized as a principle: a truth that imposes itself on the logical as well as on the metaphysical planes. We are faced, again, with a *reversal*: motherhood shifts, changes sign, from the natural side, where man has confined it, to the philosophical and logical side. This shift proceeds by analogy with the one that has seen masculine thought differentiate itself from its natural foundation, that is, by cancelling the body and the psychological life. It could be seen as a symbolic revenge (*rivalsa*), as a different use of philosophy in comparison to what man has done. But this is so only in content. Therefore, it does not leave the mind-body dualism behind, of which philosophy itself, as freedom from "the capricious domination of the real," is a consequence. The *wholeness* (*interezza*), the unity of body and mind, would not be the fruit of a *modification* of oneself as the unveiling of an interiorized vision of the world, as the first feminism had thought, but a logical truth guaranteed by the "negotiation with the mother" and a practice, such as that of "entrusting" (*affidamento*), which translates within adult life the ancient relation with the mother in order to make it live again as the principle of symbolic authority.

Thus, I conclude by saying that maintaining the centrality of motherhood means to remain—even though in a different way than the women's movement prior to the 1970s—within an emancipatory logic. That is, it confirms, rather than questioning, the representation of women as "gender," an identity in which all women should see themselves. It means to abide by a dualistic system that has built the masculine and the feminine as complementary, to limit oneself to reverse priorities and values, therefore not abandoning the dilemma of *equality-difference*, and to swing between assimilation to the masculine, seen as neutral and universal, and the preservation or valorization of feminine specificity. It means to turn "gender" into the theoretical-political paradigm of a *collective subject*.

ER You see the thought of sexual difference as a form of "emancipation" and not of "liberation." Yet, the thought of sexual difference distances itself from emancipatory feminism based on equality between man and woman and equal opportunities. Why do you consider it as a form of emancipation?

LM It is true that the thought of sexual difference, in the formulation that the Milan Women's Bookstore provided in the early 1980s, has distanced itself from emancipation. But the reconstruction provided in the book *Non credere di avere dei diritti*[33] somehow considers the 1970s feminism as characterized by issues of rights, thereby erasing the revolution represented by the practices of *autocoscienza* and of the unconscious. Motherhood returns as a "symbolic order," disconnected from the materiality of the bodies and the psychic life and as the content of a language already given, philosophy. It is therefore a theoretical construction modeled by analogy with masculine thought: the symbolic order of the mother against that of the father, feminine genealogies against the genealogy from father to son. Men are simply asked to recognize a primary order and the authority of women. The feminine as "gender" comes back, even though reinterpreted, redressed with a positive value.

ER In what you just said, there is also a critique of organized and specialized knowledge. Why? What kind of knowledge is the knowledge you have acquired through feminism? How does it differ from specialized forms of knowledge?

LM Disciplinary or specialized knowledge bears the mark of opposing separations (*separazioni oppositive*), which is at the foundation of patriarchy. In an enlightening passage, in *A Room of One's Own*, Virginia Woolf writes with clarity that women are present in the books and works of men as "a worm with eagle wings": they are exalted in imagination, but they are historically insignificant. It is a contradiction that appears much more incredible if we think that in schools—at least in Italy—women are the overwhelming majority that passes down a knowledge that they have not created. This knowledge has identified woman with the body, and at the same time woman is placed in the position of disciplining other bodies. When feminism entered the university, the practice of *autocoscienza* was the first thing to be lost, in that it undermined the very concept of "scientific rigor," understood as objectivity, as absence of "personal" interferences. Gender studies have acquired content coming from feminism, but they have brought it into disciplinary languages without questioning them as such. In the group "sexuality and writing"—also called "sexuality and the symbolic"—we had said that writing was not a means and that it was necessary to learn "to read mercilessly the writing of the unconscious in our own writings." Essentially, it was a question of inventing a new language, finding a "salvific bilingualism" (*salvifico bilinguismo*)[34] that would be "able to reason with the profound memory of oneself, the 'intimate language of infancy' and, at the same time, with the 'words from the outside,' the languages of social life, of work and of institutions." We were starting from the idea that specialized knowledge had to let itself be modified, be contaminated by "those flashes of knowledge that come from a slow modification of oneself."

ER You keep coming back to the need of a critique of dualism, of the tendency to explain and understand reality by way of binary and opposed concepts: mind-body, reason-emotion, matter-spirit, subject-object, nature-culture, humanity-animality, and so on. How do you explain that this way of thinking continues to have a hold on our thinking?

LM Currently, we hear a lot about gender binary and often in a simplistic way, as if it were just a matter of putting masks on and off. The questioning of heterosexism and heterosexuality as we have inherited them—as "natural" and "normative"—does not have a great probability of success if it does not interrogate the process of differentiation that, from the start, has identified woman with the body, with animality, and man with thought, spirituality, and history. From this point of view, we can understand that dualism is at the basis of all polarities that we know and is the foundation of our Greek-Roman-Christian culture and, in a variety of ways, all civilizations. It is a differentiation that has opposed indissoluble parts of the human and that necessarily bears inscribed within itself their reunification.

We must also not forget that gender structures relations of power and that the love dream is seen as an ideal reunification of the two divided sides of the human species. The love dream has been attributed to feminine sentimentalism, but, actually, it is born inside man's civilization, as a harmonious rejoining of what history has divided.

I think that sexual dualism—and all dualities built on top of that—has a prehistory (yet to be investigated in its depth), in the relationship of the man-son to the maternal body. This event is at the origin of every individual but tends to prolong itself beyond measure due to the *history* that has been built on it: the identification of the woman with the mother and with the sexual object. We can hypothesize that, in attributing to women the natural destiny of sexuality and motherhood—because this is the legacy of the Greek-Roman-Christian culture—man has fixated his experience as a child on the body that generated him. The figure of the woman as an *erotic and maternal body* is drawn, first of all, from the imaginary of birth. The son perceives its *power*, and the adult man reverses the relationship of originary dependence by submitting and turning to his advantage the attractive sides he has seen in woman. If masculine sexuality appears so meager, reduced to consumption, to performance, it is also because man has shifted to woman the possibility of pleasure, of being desirable—her own sexuality—while reserving for himself force, power, and money in order to reappropriate them. This opens the possibility for women to avail themselves of their *attractions* as power and value precisely in order to be recognized. This means that the recurring and everlasting figures of the feminine—the *seductress*, the *mother*—are inscribed with the power man has seen in the mother's body, as well as his own devaluation and subjugation.

The feminism of the 1970s has confronted this vision of the world at its roots and has done so through the practice of *autocoscienza* pushed to its depths, to the border with unconscious formations. The return to the logic of gender, even if revisited in terms of positivity, has slowed down the process of liberation from the masculine and feminine figures. It is only since the year 2000 that we have again started to critically question dualism, what it has represented in the relationship between the sexes but also in fixing roles, identities, and sexual choices in a normative way. The openness of the new feminist generation—Non Una Di Meno—to LGBTQ+ subjectivities has been another step forward toward change.

ER   You have spoken of the feminine as a construction by the masculine, the product of man's gaze that sees woman in relation to himself, taken as the measure and the norm. Do you think that this feminine is still alive in the present world? The Me Too movement in the US has publicly denounced the masculine domination and has shown how it disposes of women's bodies. Do you think that this movement may be able to eliminate the feminine as expression of masculine domination?

LM   I start with an obvious observation. Women have been excluded from the polis for centuries, but the same can be said of "femininity," of the social and cultural construction of the feminine "gender," by the representation that man—the only protagonist of history—has provided of the other sex. In the course of civilization, man has imposed norms and roles to control and shape destiny to his own advantage, naming it according to his fears and desires. In the metaphoric and symbolic use that has been made of femininity, the feminine swings between opposite poles, now identified with nature—matter, animality—now with the dream of a transhuman purity, as if, in woman, man had seen both his *damnation* and his *salvation*.

Even though the images of the feminine are many, as we can see from books of art and literature, however, they gravitate essentially toward two stereotypes: the one that goes back to the material root of the human and to the natural drives, seen as guilt, sin, or as a regenerating force, and the one that should sustain man in his need for spiritualization. In this imaginary that swings between earth and sky, returning to primordial instincts and moral elevation, projected on woman, we can read the dilemma of dualism that has kept man divided in himself—between body and thought. This is the outcome of the violent differentiation that has left woman to represent the material origin of the human while man became the material origin of history.

The feminine as the specter of man's desires and fears has become the historical and cultural identity of woman. If it has prevented women from grasping a more real perception of themselves, it is because it has been not only imposed from the outside, but it is also a representation of the world that women have internalized and made their own. One is woman, but it is as if she always has to discover it. This means that we are confronted with a historical construction of "gender" that has become "naturalized."

The feminine is constructed by man's gaze, in relation to and in function of man; it is in relation to man insofar as he places himself as the "measure," the "norm" of the human in its full sense—body and thought—and dictates in what ways the other sex "differs." What it "lacks" is in function of man in that the feminine acquires sense and existence only in its devotion to the other, in ensuring the good of the other.

The Me Too movement has uncovered what we already knew about the abuses and the extortions that women suffer in the workplace, and it is important that it is women themselves who brought this out. Since it involved celebrities known to the public, the risk of voyeurism and media trials were present, at the beginning at least. Besides this, I think that a denunciation is not enough. There remains, above all, the initiative of an individual woman that does not take on a collective action. It is necessary to reflect, at the same time, on how women themselves, forcibly, turn their attractiveness into an exchange currency for success, money, and career.

ER When you speak of feminine roles imposed by masculine domination—seductress, mother—you say that women have internalized this model of femininity to a point that they lend themselves often to these roles of wife-lover with devotion. They feel indispensable in their function as if everything were to crumble without them. Would you explain this mechanism of power that subjugates to the point of not leaving any room for thinking otherwise? How does one leave behind this kind of enslavement/survival that pervades every aspect of a life to its innermost depths?

LM I have often asked myself: what kind of feminine is the one we see on stage? Are the bodies that invade the media liberated bodies or prostituted bodies? What is the relation between this "femininity" that is exalted as a resource, as "added value," and real women? From what emerges by carefully observing the representation of the media—research, publications, newspaper articles—but even by what we have before our eyes daily, there is no doubt that there is a *return in force to gender stereotypes*. This is seen particularly in the representation of woman as an *erotic body and a body that generates*, in other words, the seductress and motherhood. *Mother* and *prostitute* are the two faces with which the classical Western (Greek and Christian) culture has considered woman's "nature," namely *sexuality*.

One could say that women are pushed to use their bodies as power since, up to now, they have not possessed anything else. The winning card for success, career, or marriage becomes physical beauty, the body as a shortcut for social recognition. But if it is the *erotic body*, exhibited, commodified, that shocks and outrages us the most, we cannot forget that no less celebrated, even though in different ways and in different contexts, is the *maternal body*.

If emancipation traditionally understood meant to conform to the masculine order, the *escape from a discredited feminine*, currently it is *the feminine that emancipates itself as such*. Woman, the body, sexuality take their revenge on the history that has excluded and erased them. Yet at the very moment women appear in the public space, the signs that this history has left on them become more evident. One realizes that "gendered" figures are much more than an imposed script: it is the only way women have had to be recognized, loved, or hated. However, the transition from a suffered condition—in that it was imposed by way of power, law, and survival—to the possibility of actively assuming it is not without meaning. No matter how questionable and perverse this is, we must admit that it is a form of *emancipation*. To speak of "choice" does not mean, however, that one is "free to choose." Thus, when reflecting on women who offer their bodies in exchange for careers and money, who make themselves "object" of the masculine gaze, who enter as exchange currency in relations among men, who put feelings and emotions and their entire life to work, I would not speak of them as "victims."

ER   Is there a feminine subjectivity beyond the feminine? On what is it founded and how does it manifest itself? If women are mired in the feminine as you have said, how do they come to their own subjectivity? How do we distinguish the feminine subjugated body from the liberated female body?

LM   What feminine subjectivity might be like beyond the models that have been imposed on women, we don't know. The real woman does not exist but, as with the "state of nature" of which Rousseau speaks, it was necessary to think it to understand how many thrills civilization had placed on it.

If we want to get closer to an authentic sense of oneself, we need to have the courage to analyze the many ways in which women have sought to survive, have faced their roles, and have assumed the imposed models while ensuring some pleasure and power: adaptations, resistances, compensations, substitutive power. The first and most lasting venue is certainly that of *making oneself indispensable to others*. It is the counterpart of the amount of gratuitous work women continue to do in their homes, such as work of care and household work. They are *substitutive powers* that remain for a great part *unnamable*, just as *love*, the dream of intimate belonging to another being. This also explains the temptation that women have to consider "care"—a maternal devotion that extends to perfectly self-sufficient adults—as a trait of their identity, their "difference," their mission in the world, instead of a collective responsibility of men and women.

In order to induce women to leave aside the centrality of the body and of love, of the seductive maternal power—no longer being "slaves that tempt to render others slaves" as Virginia Woolf wrote—awareness is not enough. It is also necessary to change the institutions of public life, of powers, of knowledge and languages that are structured in light of traditional gender differences. It is above all necessary that men, instead of making women their objects, using them and protecting them, begin to pull their mask of *neutrality* down. It is necessary that men question themselves, their fears and their desires, the culture produced by centuries of masculine domination, recognizing how little room for choice they have had as well, in having to wear the manly armor.

ER   What does feminist liberation mean for men?

LM Since its origins, the birth of patriarchy can be read as a form of emancipation. The "father principle," writes Bachofen in *Matriarcato* (*Myth, Religion, and Mother Right*),[35] is spiritual, immortal, and released from matter, mortality, and biology of which woman is the depositary as the body that generates, as fecund earth. The historical community of men can be read as an escape from the feminine and from everything that it has represented up to now, as a hierarchic imposition of values and powers. Taking into account that the differentiation between masculine and feminine destiny modeled all other dualities we know of—body and thought, nature and culture, feelings and reason, and so on—one can say that men inherit from their fathers a privilege, but also a profound mutilation as far as essential experiences of the human are concerned. Although they have thought of themselves as individuals, relegating woman to a "gender," it is evident that virility is a cultural and social construction as well, a script integrated and seen as "natural," which is not easy to sustain, not even by men.

I would not use the adjective "feminist," if not with reference to the feminist practice of "starting from oneself." Yet we can certainly speak of "liberation" for men as well, in the sense that it is not only a question of losing powers and privileges, but also of welcoming within themselves human experiences, perhaps the most creative, that they have projected onto the other sex, thereby continuing to make them the object of both desire and fear.

ER You have founded, together with other women, the Libera Università delle Donne (LUD, Free University of Women) in Milan,[36] of which you are now the president. Tell us about this place: how it was thought, how it came to be, and whatever else you think we should know about it.

LM The experience of the "150-hour course" in via Gabbro, as well as the pioneering commitment of some of the women that had tenaciously wanted it, expanded in other areas of Milan, and this meant that, at the end of 1970s, there were around two thousand women enrolled in these courses. To preserve the work that had involved so many women, we decided, in 1987, to create an association that would ensure its continuity beyond the school. The "Free University of Women" was thus born out of the desire of women who had met as teachers and students. It has celebrated its thirty years of life not too long ago. At the beginning, we decided to maintain the teacher–student relationship but with the intention of gradually moving to group reflection, without the need of a teacher. In part, it has been so.

Currently, LUD's activities are various: courses, seminars, reading groups, experiential writing workshops, and courses on video, music, and theater apprenticeship. But at its foundation, the unifying element is that of starting from our lives and questioning the given knowledge and the given languages to arrive at a new language capable of—as we said in 1978 in the "writing and the symbolic" group—"disrupting, in the writing of women, the ways of thinking and of expression acquired without having the freedom of choosing" (*sconvolgere, nella scrittura delle donne, i modi di pensare e di esprimersi acquisiti senza che si avesse la libertà di scegliere*).[37] It is about rethinking issues in a place free from academic rules and conditionings, free from established forms of knowledge, and doing so in the outskirts (*periferie*), which have always been abandoned. Many collections have gathered lessons and personal writings from the courses. The material that has been produced is enormous. There are also a number of books, among them *Verifica d'identità* (Verification of identity), *Donne del Nord/Donne del Sud* (Women of the North/Women of the South), *Cocktail d'amore* (Love cocktail), *Scienziate nel tempo* (Women scientists over time), *Incontrare la vecchiaia* (Encounters with old age), *In punta di piedi nel conflitto* (On one's toes in a conflict), *Lungo la strada* (Along the road). Reflections on war, on biotechnologies, on the new languages of technology and of social networks, on violence against women, on lesbianism, on the relationship with women who are not Italian, with feminisms in the world, and so on, are the great themes at the center. My only regret is that there has not been as much exchange with women working in the universities as we had expected: exchanges between the inside and the outside of institutions of learning, that is, a sort of a commute from one place to the other. Communication happens even in the forms offered by the new technologies: since 2002, we have an active website that today represents a veritable archive of reflections and initiatives, and a vivacious Facebook page.

Over the years, a leap forward has overcome two pivotal aspects of the previous work: that of the relationship teacher–student, and that of a plurality and a heterogeneity that are often difficult to bring to the outside. We want to give life to a place of a multiplicity of knowledge, a place that has the force and the goal to reach outside, and that speaks on current issues. As a method of relationship for the work done in the groups and in the courses, we rely on exchanges without hierarchal divisions between those who know and those who don't and do our work showing respect for individual competences and research choices. Our courses turn almost always into a collective endeavor where everyone has knowledge and the words to convey it.

It is a beautiful story and a story of passions. It is not a little venture. It is one that speaks of the new horizons of Italian feminism. The question is: How do we transform such a force, so much awareness, so much accumulated knowledge, into words through which to take part in the world and with which to make one's own position matter? We know that it is difficult, but it is a crucial task. For those who have seen the Free University of Women come to life, this has been a commitment and a duty also toward one's own history. For the young women who are joining women's politics now, it is an opportunity not to be missed. It is not simple to create something like this, to give it life by respecting all diversities. We view it as an undertaking of political responsibility (*un'assunzione di responsabilità politica*). In 2002, the association received an attestation of merit from the city of Milan. A few years earlier, I also received a similar recognition—*l'ambrogino d'oro*—as a "feminist theorist."

ER You have used the expression "off topic" to describe your life: a life lived outside a woman's predetermined destiny. To change the world, is it necessary that more women—and more men—live a life "off topic"?

LM I have used the expression "off topic" only to indicate all those experiences of the human, the most universal experiences, that have remained outside culture, history, and politics as traditionally understood. I knew by experience of the violence I had witnessed in my family, of the poverty and of the exploitation of peasant labor and I put all of it in a piece that was supposed to be literary. "Very well written, but off topic" was the teacher's judgment. It is true that, having used it often, it has been extended to my life as a whole—a life certainly anomalous, compared to what is traditionally expected of a woman. Since I arrived in Milan in 1966, I have always lived alone, in very small, rented apartments and in precarious economic conditions, having left the school system early to devote myself fully to the women's movement. Aside from some brief love relationships, which never became cohabitations, I have always faced what I call *singolitudine* (singleness) with the profound conviction that it was precociously inscribed in my life, but that I could turn it slowly into a "necessary virtue," chosen out of destiny. My book *Come nasce il sogno d'amore* talks essentially about this: how to exit from the "long slumber" that keeps the human tied to the originary experience of fusion with the body that has generated him or her, tied to a dream of complementarity that makes us see, in the different sex, the completion of ourselves, as if we were two halves of a whole. Arriving at the albeit "fastidious obligation to live by oneself," as Aleramo calls it, remains an important experience, in my view, even for those who live as a couple, for those who have children. It is a way of avoiding creating obligations of indispensability and dependence where they are not necessary. To give voice to what has been for so long "unsayable" means to open perspectives that have remained unthought in comparison to rigid models that are often dehumanizing.

ER How is current feminism, compared to the feminism of the 1970s? Is there something that was not there in the 1970s or that was there then, but not today? Do you think that feminism might become redundant over time?

LM In the course of half a century, I have seen different generations of feminism appear on the public scene. Every time, I have welcomed them with enthusiasm, hoping they would last. It has not always been the case and, every time, I have consoled myself by saying that the women's movement is the only movement that has survived the 1970s and has a karstic evolution (*andamento carsico*).[38] Then, in 2016, starting in Argentina, the network Non Una Di Meno (NUDM) arrived. Besides being an international movement, like the feminism of the 1970s, NUDM is in continuity with what was the ambitious challenge of feminism at that earlier time, namely the "modification of oneself and of the world": to start from personal life and from the history that has been buried and naturalized for centuries, to rethink patriarchy and all forms of domination to which patriarchy has given a foundation, including capitalism. In the document promoting the demonstration on the 24th of November 2017, in Rome, it was written: "We are the change. . . . We want to transform society, the entire world," we demonstrate against "male violence toward gender and racism and against the governments that legitimize it." The links (*nessi*) that in the 1970s we were hoping to find between sexuality and politics, between sexuality and economy, sexuality and the symbolic, are today out in the open and at the center of a "permanent unrest" by a young generation of women and other subjects—LGBQT+—that have filled the squares for over two years, have held local and national rallies, and have interrogated themselves on the intersection of class, sex, race, religion, among others. We owe them credit for an extraordinary feminist agenda against male violence on women and against gender violence. They go beyond power relationships between sexes. They are attentive to domination and exploitation in all their historical manifestations.

What I currently see confirms that the impossible, the real that is only intuited in a specific historical phase, becomes possible in another phase that comes later. In NUDM, I have seen, with pleasure and not without emotion, the revival of the complex articulation of issues raised by feminism, and this currently goes under the name of *intersectionality*: the thematization of the ties between sexism, classism, nationalism, fascism, and homo- and transphobia.

If feminism can be considered itself the main reference for a process of liberation shared by many subjectivities, it is because its practices—starting from oneself, attention to the body, feelings, imaginary, unconscious formation, questioning those needs that are cultivated by the dominant apparatus—allow us to question the contradictions that open up when sex, gender, race, class, and so on, are seen as part of the lived experience and of individual experience. We know that it is possible to be, at the same time, anti-capitalist, and sexist, and homophobic. The unifying element is to be found, in my view, in the radical practices with which feminism has sought to redefine politics: the centrality of the personal and of relationships, the critique of every dualism, the invention of a language capable of "reasoning both in terms of the profound memory of oneself—the intimate language of childhood—and in terms of the words from the outside—the languages of social life, of work, and of institutions."

I do not believe that feminism could become redundant soon. What we still need—and the new generation is not so inclined to practice this—is self-reflection, digging into one's life, into the unconscious formations that, for centuries, have maintained the only representation of the world we have inherited. While anti-capitalism and anti-racism have a history, sexism—which I consider the originary substructure (*impianto*) of every form of domination—is, not surprisingly, the last one to arrive at some awareness, and the first one to disappear. One reason for this is to be found in the perverse intertwining of masculine power and intimate life.

ER Beyond your feminist commitment, your love for reading and writing, what are your other passions? What do you love doing?

LM This is a question that embarrasses me and makes me laugh a little. I admit that feminism, as a practice and as thought, has been my sole and my full-time passion. The only distractions have been dancing—my parents in Romagna were two exceptional dancers—and cinema—it captures me immediately, as a rapture, only by a few shots. After leaving teaching, feminism has meant for me a collective commitment made of meetings, conferences, workshops in different cities, a pleasant mix—although sometimes tiring—of holidays, dinners, walks, and work. I sometimes think of myself as a "social solitary" precisely because of the alternation of intellectually and emotionally intense moments and long periods when I remain alone in my apartment. It is small, but full of light, with a view on the roofs of Milan, a long balcony full of vines and flowers, and, sometimes, a passing blackbird.

But there is another passion that has come late and suddenly. It is the discovery of an island to which I have returned every summer since 1975. I went there after a conference organized by the University of Cagliari with my feminist friends. There I heard of the beauty of this island, and I went on vacation with "some" women friends—which ended up being about two hundred. It was an experience that left a mark: sun, swims, meetings, animated discussions, dances, dinners, and an unusual everydayness.

For me, who grew up in the country, the discovery of the sea has been like a new birth, also considering that I had never learned to swim. I started to move in those deep waters as if they were my natural element. Since then, I have returned there every summer, in the same beautiful house that I rent and share with some women friends, more or less as loyal as myself. For my love of the island and for having participated in their song festivals in addition to the short poetic fragments I have dedicated to the island, I have been given "honorary citizenship." As I say often, Carloforte—that is the name of the island—is my love dream realized, unique and perfect, a happiness that is renewed every time I return.

ER Looking from the outside at everything that you continue doing, there is no doubt that you have had the life you have chosen for yourself. This must be very rewarding. Is there something specific you're proud of? Do you regret not having done something or not having done something differently?

LM I cannot deny it, I have done what I have desired: carrying forth the passions that have changed my life, the encounter with the non-authoritarian movements of the 1970s, continuing my studies, my writings, and my political commitment, full-time and in freedom. If I had not devoted all my time and energies to feminism, I would have not seen realized the projects that I have loved, such as the periodical *Lapis* and the Free University of Women, besides my books that were all born from the relationships I have had with women in various cities or, in the case of the advice column (*posta del cuore*), with teenagers who sent me their letters. I have had the life I have chosen. Even when, later in life, my poverty—propertyless and daughter of the propertyless—began to weigh on me, above all in terms of the need for some care I could not afford, I have not had any doubt or second thought. I have always lived on my own. I have learned what it means to look after the ill body of an old person you love, in the eight years my mother was infirm, after my father died. Those were very difficult years, with crises of panic due to economic precariousness and fatigue, mine, hers, in a small town that I no longer knew after leaving it when I was twenty-five. It was now a wealthier town, but more selfish than how I had known it in the past. If there is something of which I am proud it is to have looked after my mother, in all the needs of her sick body, to have brought her closer to me as a woman, and to have accompanied her in this painful, last journey of life. I think I owe her much—besides her talents as a dancer, the cheerfulness with which she welcomed everyone, her generosity, and her lively sense of humor, something she never lacked. I regret only not having danced as much as she wished me to.

ER Your writing and your thinking are in a way like a dance, I would say. Are you working on something at the moment? Any future projects?

LM The only book I have "worked" on with continuity and for eight long years was *Come nasce il sogno d'amore*. The other ones were born along the way, between moments of solitude and encounters with other women, and they are, not surprisingly, collections of articles, essays, brief annotations. Generally, this is how it happens. After a journey that can last a few years, in which different commitments interlace, such as meetings with feminist groups, newspaper articles, interviews, participation in conferences, readings, I retrace my steps and I find the thread that connects the writings I have left behind. For someone like me, who has one single passion, thinking moves in ongoing and continual revisits (*continue riprese*) and variations on the same theme. In the preface of my book *Lo strabismo della memoria*, I wrote that, for me, the book was "the point of intersection between a long research work, subject to changes, to stops, to unexpected revisits and the idea that secretly guided it. . . . This makes us think that the book is not where we look for it: in the orderly sequence of reasonings or in the effort of an accurate linguistic construction, and, even less, in the a priori project that seems to contain it and give it meaning."[39]

There has never been a book in my future, not even when the future was still a line stretched out into the infinite. It is even less so today, when the future is counted in years. To be honest, however, I secretly harbor in my thoughts, even though not so secretly since it surfaces often, the idea of a provocative booklet, which perhaps I will not have the courage to write. There is a book that I keep reading and have reread at various times, every time transcribing fragments of it, as it is my habit. It is *Sesso e carattere* by the Viennese philosopher Otto Weininger,[40] who died suicidal at only twenty-three, in 1903, a few months after the publication of this book, which was much discussed and reprinted many times. Every time I read it, I say: "Weininger is right," and immediately after: "How can a feminist say that a racist sexist is right?" In his vision, Weininger said what we, with less awareness, have learned and transmitted in schools, with the Greek-Roman-Christian culture, a vision of the world that we have internalized, men and women, and that is still part of high culture and common sense. If I ever write such a book, I will have to find a less provocative title, something like: "Weininger's Reason: A Dialogue between a Feminist and a Misogynist."

ER I realize that the questions I have asked do not exhaust your experience as a woman, as a feminist, and of your work as a whole. Is there something in particular that you find relevant that you would like to add?

LM I have never loved autobiographies. Maybe it is because, as I have said often, I belong to those who have no history, such as women and peasants. Perhaps it is also because my memory of the past has shipwrecked due to much suffering, so much so that to open up even a slim path toward the twenty-five years spent in the small town of my origins, I have needed the words of others, those who seemed to have written for me as well, or those who could act as my counterfigures (*controfigura*): fragments of *autocoscienza* through a third party (*per interposta persona*). I consider this interview and conversation a particularly happy experience. Not only does it not leave out any important moment in my personal and political life, but it is also as if the questions had taken me with ease, profound understanding, and affection, and accompanied me in a journey that could only be a weaving of threads. This is what I have always thought that the experiential writing should be, namely, a wandering that draws its order from the prehistory on which it has built itself, without its knowing. I'd like to think that, for some mystery of life, your last name, Roncalli, has something to do with it, your kinship with someone you have not known, but who has been of great help during my hard adolescence and youth in the small town where I grew up.

ER Thank you, Lea, for your kind words.

Luisa Muraro. The author thanks Luisa Muraro for the photo and kind permission to include it in this volume.

Luisa Muraro was born in 1940 in Montecchio Maggiore near Vicenza, Italy, the sixth of eleven children. She lives in Milan. She studied philosophy at the Catholic University of Milan where she began her academic career, which was interrupted early by the protests of 1968. Soon thereafter she became involved with the feminist movement through Lia Cigarini of the DEMAU group. She has remained faithful to the originary feminism, which would later be called the "feminism of difference," and which has inspired a great part of her subsequent work. From 1976 to 2006 she taught philosophy at the University of Verona where, in 1983, she created with other women the philosophical community Diotima. To this day, she remains a collaborator of its website (www.diotimafilosofe.it). She is one of the founding members of the Milan Women's Bookstore (1975), and a curator, with other women, of its magazine *Via Dogana* and its website (www.libreriadelledonne.it). She has participated in various international conferences—such as in Chicago (1997), in Santiago, Chile (1998), in Sana'a, Yemen (1999)—and has presented on the ideas of Italian feminism. She has taught as part of the master's program Estudios de la Libertad Femenina at the University of Barcelona, promoted by the group Duoda. Her written work includes many titles, among them books, conference papers, and articles in journals, newspapers, and on the internet. Among her most recent publications is a biographical interview, *Non si può insegnare tutto* by Riccardo Fanciullacci (La Scuola 2013). Some of her essays are included in the collection *Another Mother*, edited by Cesare Casarino and Andrea Righi (University of Minnesota Press 2018). *The Symbolic Order of the Mother* (State University of New York Press 2018) is the best known of her political-philosophical works.

Two

"But I Am a Woman"

Sexual Difference as Subjective Truth
("Ma io sono una donna":
differenza sessuale come verità soggettiva)

In Conversation with Luisa Muraro

Elvira Roncalli In looking at the long list of your publications, one has the immediate impression of finding oneself before a woman of letters, a writer and a thinker who has devoted herself to scrutinizing history, literature, and philosophy; a woman who moves elegantly and incisively between times far gone and the present, and who gives us stories that are perhaps not well known. I am thinking, for example, of *Guglielma e Maifreda*, and of *La signora del gioco*, and of *Le Amiche di Dio: Margherita e le altre* (2001).[1] Do you see yourself in this characterization of a woman intellectual and scholar? In what sense does this description speak of you and in what sense does it overlook or leave out important aspects of yourself and of your work?

Luisa Muraro I do not see myself in the character of a woman intellectual and scholar as portrayed in your question; but I admit that this may be said of me, even though approximately and from the outside. As it has happened to other people, I am someone who has been charged by historical and biographical circumstances with the task of putting into words what has changed and is changing with feminism, myself included. I have watched myself changing from the inside out by way of a surprising correspondence between what was happening and what I desired, without knowing this in advance. "Feminism" is a label; to say the thing in question in the right words is part of the assignment that I have received. I have responded in the ways I have at my disposal. Among these: that I am able to reason well, that I am eloquent, and that I have had a good education. All of this explains why I may be seen, as you say, as a scholar and an intellectual, yet my motives and my stance do not correspond to this. For instance, among my motives was the desire to satisfy my mother's desire to do well in school. She was the daughter of a teacher in a small town; only her brothers were permitted to study, whereas she was only able to complete mandatory education. In pursuing my studies, I was also pursuing my mother's denied desire and vindicating it. The modern intellectual is presumed to be an adult male who has broken his ties of dependence from his parents. In myself though, these ties have not been broken and when I became aware of this, I gave up other dependencies but kept the one related to my mother's desire.

  I have carried out the task of naming what has changed and is changing with feminism, and I continue to do so. I have carried out this task on my own terms, which are not only mine. Among my terms there are also some limitations, obviously, and also the conditions dictated by the task itself. Among these, I consider it fundamental not to separate myself (the subject) from the thing in question, feminism. I cannot be objective, I must keep open the passage between inside and outside, which I call "the inner passage." Under certain circumstances, this may seem difficult or above and beyond my capacity. In these cases, failing is better than conforming. I leave to intuition the fact that there is also an inner passage, beyond my reasoning and the facts. This is the only way I know to keep myself and feminism in that correspondence, preventing its deterioration into a label, similar to the correspondence that exists, for instance—and which I like—between a surfer and the sea.

ER You just said that you do not find yourself in the character of a woman intellectual and scholar. How would you describe yourself?

LM I cannot describe myself. I understand that others may see me as an intellectual and a scholar because of the books I have written, and I will admit that I do not dislike being seen that way. But I do not recognize myself in that character.

ER You speak of feminism as a task that you have received. In what sense do you call it a "task"?

LM I mean to say that circumstances have placed me in front of a decision I had to make. When I understood that—and I understood it early—I did not hesitate, and I never regretted my feminist choice. It did not feel like a duty, but I recognized it as my task.

ER Truth passes through the subject and that is why you cannot be objective, you just said. What problems do you see with objectivity?

LM Objectivity is not claimed in the first person. It is an entire symbolic device that says what objectivity is to you, that preaches it, that makes you understand it. But it is not an individual man or an individual woman who decides. The feminist choice—because this is what I'm talking about—is a decision about which I have no hesitation or personal doubts. This is why I speak of a "task" that I have received. I did not give it to myself; it is not just one's own choice. Men speak of "mission," but this is not a way of speaking that corresponds to me. It is a task, not a mission.

ER In hearing you talk about this, the word "vocation" comes to mind.

LM Oh yes, that could be. The word "vocation" is familiar to me—one of my brothers had a religious vocation when he was very young—but having said this, I like the word "task" better.

ER How would you describe your work as a whole?

LM My work is all about teaching what I have found out gradually in pursuing (my) research. The word I use, *insegnare*, besides the meaning of the English equivalent, "to teach," in Italian also means "showing" and "to show," for example, "to show the path," and in my language, the two meanings are joined together. I do not teach without showing the path that I am taking and without showing the paths that open up as we go. My work teaches some paths and teaches how to look for them. These are paths that do not transcend the mediations possible through practice; that is to say, they are within the language and the languages that human beings speak among themselves. However, if a path opens up that I cannot take, such as an aesthetic or a mystical path, I teach it in the sense of showing it as best I can, but nothing more. Overall, my research does not fit exactly into this or that subject matter or discipline and does not ever become specialized. The Western philosophical tradition authorizes me to do so.

Another question stemming from your question: Is there something that ties the research itself from within and that gives cohesion to the outcome, namely the work? In what I do, I try to bring to light the greatness of the unexplored dimension of the difference of being a woman. It is my very own same greatness, given that I am also what is called a woman. Given that I have turned this "I am a woman" into my own sign, I therefore call myself a feminist. It is a greatness that must stand out independently from the already established measures, in that these do not correspond happily to what a woman truly desires. The greatness of a man also does not fit within preestablished measures, someone may object. I think so too; still, I am a woman.

ER What do you mean when you say that "the philosophical tradition authorizes you to do so"?

LM Let's think of Spinoza, or of Montaigne, or of Thomas Aquinas. They are all figures with very different situations, but if one is called to philosophize, one can do it, whatever his or her condition. It is only in the nineteenth century that philosophy becomes an academic discipline; it was not one before. Let's think also of Socrates . . .

ER Thus, you see philosophy as free thinking, as thinking.

LM Yes, of course, with its own discipline, its own requirements, but it is free thinking.

ER The philosophical tradition as a knowledge that has been handed down and that is based on a canon is, however, in many ways, limiting and restrictive.

LM No. What is philosophy? I have looked for an answer and this is what I found: philosophy is to fight with words so that something true is said, that is to say, to fight with words in order to put into words what presents itself as true to me.

ER You said that your work tries to say and put into words the "greatness" of woman. Of what does this greatness consist?

LM Everything that a woman is able to be, often without even thinking about it, often without even knowing it, often even doubting it—I don't know what to call this, except greatness. It is about thinking that humanity is the feminine work by definition. Women do it, they are it, they are humanity. This is the greatness of being a woman. The human being that we call woman is a very great thing, and it is a greatness, for the most part, unexplored. "Man" with the capital "M," we know what his greatness consists of, and I think that every man—I think of my son, for instance—knows what I mean when I say: "Be a man." By contrast, for a woman, her greatness is another dimension; I am not saying completely different from man, but a version of the human that is not explored. I like to explore that dimension in itself and not insofar as it resembles man.

ER As a continent all to be discovered?

LM Not exactly. This is Freud's expression. Woman is not a continent but a human being in a dimension that is other, yet to be discovered.

ER Your books, your articles, and essays are many. There appears a clear preference for women of the past and also—something that may surprise someone who does not know your work well—many writings on women mystics, such as *Lingua materna, scienza divina: Scritti sulla filosofia mistica di Margherita Porete, Le amiche di Dio: Scritti di mistica femminile, Le amiche di Dio: Margherita e le altre*.[2] Tell us about your love for women mystics to whom you devote much of your work. Where does it come from? What moves you toward them? What is the relationship between these women, their writings, and your work?

LM I came to the movement of the beguines[3] through research on a Milanese heretical group at the end of the thirteenth century. This research enabled me to meet Romana Guarnieri of the Edizioni di Storia e Letteratura and, guided by her, I came to the movement of the beguines. Without her and without Paul Verdeyen of the Ruusbroec Center in Antwerp, Belgium—both very generous—I would not have discovered the existence of Marguerite Porete and of the other theologians in their mother tongue—as it seems more fitting to call the women mystic writers of the Middle Ages. In the year 2000, considering the fifteen years I had spent on these studies, I asked myself: What was I thinking of doing or of finding in these writings, so far away in time, and outside my competence? I remembered a dream in which I was crying because I had committed to do something I did not know how to do. It was the story of my philosophical vocation repeating itself. To the question, I answered: "I have looked for what I am not up to, for what is out of my depths." As a matter of fact, from the women mystics I have learned that unpreparedness is the way to make being be, to give life to life. What does this mean? Not being up to it, knowing it, and yet being able to be there—this is the intelligence of love, the intellect of love, says Dante.

If I were given a second life, I would devote myself to the book of Marguerite, known as Porete. The scholars in these disciplines, such as the German Kurt Ruh and the American Bernard McGinn, of the Divinity School at the University of Chicago, consider her book, *Le mirouer des simples âmes*,[4] a masterpiece, maybe the greatest of Western mysticism in the vernacular. I need a second life in order to give consistence of words and ideas to my admiration for Marguerite's book and the context out of which it flourished. At the center of the book, yet to be written, will be the culmination of the research by women mystics. They start from a sense of not being up to and they arrive at saying, with Marguerite, "mon manque est mon mieux"—"that which I lack is my best."[5]

But first, in this life, is the commitment to becoming independent from the dominant culture—lay or religious, clerical or anticlerical—and finding the language to give meaning to the greatness of these women called beguines. An impossible goal? I do not agree. The symbolic independence is a possible gain for both men and women. In this, we women are aided by that *estrangement* about which Virginia Woolf speaks in *Three Guineas*. Luce Irigaray, in her turn, has given us an example of religious unscrupulousness in *Femmes divines*, a 1984 conference published in *Sexes et parentés* (*Sexes and Genealogies*).[6] For me and other scholars, her example had the value of authorizing us to turn our look toward that *somewhere else and otherwise* that we ourselves are and did not dare to tell ourselves because of patriarchy.

ER About the women mystics, or the women theologians in their mother tongue, as you refer to them, what they teach you is that they start by saying they are not up to and arrive at saying with Marguerite Porete that *mon manque est mon mieux*, "that which I lack is my best."

LM Yes, these are the very words of Marguerite Porete and they are words of extraordinary depth.

ER Tell us more about this: a lack, which can be thought also as estrangement, is actually something that is more, a surplus.

LM It is the opening onto the absolute, onto the infinite. There is an entire episode that talks about this. Marguerite is talking to her Love—rarely does she call her God—and she asks her (Love) to give her (Marguerite) the capacity she finds in her (Love)—Love in the French of her time is feminine—her capacity to love, her divine capacity to love. Marguerite knows that this is what she lacks and so she asks Love for it. But Love answers, "I can't," and Marguerite protests saying: "When we made our friendship pact, you said 'everything that is mine is yours,' but I lack something that you have and that you don't want to give to me." Love answers: "I can't," and she (Love) offers Marguerite other things in exchange. Suddenly, Marguerite says harshly: "Be quiet! Don't say anything more. Now I have understood. *Mon manque est mon mieux.*" That which I lack is my best. Why? Because it is a lack of being that calls being, therefore constantly receiving being. It is a profound thought, and she is able to render it in this episode, which unfortunately in the translation that we have is mistaken—as I said, I will devote my next life to the book on Marguerite. She says *mon manque est mon mieux* as a discovery. It is the discovery of the ontological radicality of desire in the human being, a desire for "nothingness," boundless, and without fulfillment.

ER In what sense is the translation mistaken?

LM In the translation of the *Mirror of Simple Souls*, as it has been handed down to us, there is a mistake. The mistake goes back to the French version that replaces the original French, now lost; but it is not found in the first Latin and English versions of the original, which were completed before the original French version was lost. The mistake consists in considering the desire for love, the love of love, the culmination of the mystical journey. The breakthrough found by Marguerite is lost. Traditionally, the mystical journey ends in the fusion with God, whereas Marguerite succeeds in finding the way to save the duality between the human being in her finitude and the divine being, in relationship with one another, because her lack of being calls for being. The relationship of the creature with the divine being comes first. God is conceived as perennial creation, that is, the perennial gift of being. Thus, the way that opens up for Marguerite is characteristic of her theology in her mother tongue, reliant on research through practice, on revelation and on reasoning.

ER Therefore, you see in this breakthrough the way toward symbolic independence. In the sense that women mystics teach you and show you symbolic independence . . .

LM Yes. It is a daring and risky operation, going from one civilization to another, but it can be done especially when and if the original language resists a literal translation. In contrast to a certain contemporary thought, I think that symbolic independence is possible; that is to say, it is possible to conceive of oneself independently from the devices of power. Since we are within a religious theme, obedience to necessity as the condition for the symbolic independence from the dominant power is precisely what Saint Paul teaches in his Letter to the Romans. There are historical moments when it is possible to see the symbolic independence of the human being. I have seen it and lived it with and through feminism, in the act of a peaceful separation that has given life to the groups of feminine *autocoscienza*[7]—consciousness raising—necessary for signifying something that could not be signified otherwise.

ER Besides mystics, which other philosophers and writers, men and women, have been and continue to be a point of reference for you? For what reasons?

LM The women who devoted themselves to mystical research belong to the area of *philosophia extra philosophiam*, that is to say, they are outside the philosophical canon, and they are not the only ones. Clarice Lispector with *A paixão segundo G.H.*,[8] Emily Dickinson with her magnificent body of poems play an important part, as do other women. I also consider close to this group those thinkers who belong completely to the philosophical canon but have not had a following corresponding to their thought and, in this sense, they are eccentric: they do not occupy a central position in the development of modernity. I think in particular of two who are found in the transition from the Middle Ages to Modern Europe: Michel de Montaigne and Nicholas of Cusa.

Rather than giving you a list, I prefer to talk about the criteria by which I feel indebted to certain authors, women and men.

I am indebted to those who have authorized me to think what I already had in mind, but which I did not dare to make my own, or with those who have opened my mind to unthought ideas. At times, it happens that the latter make me discover things, and then I say to myself: but I already knew these things and I had "forgotten" them. Plato, as is known, was inspired by a similar experience of recollection. I can say that something similar has happened to me regarding the feminist writers whom I have read, such as Kate Millet, Carla Lonzi, and Adrienne Rich. They have written very new things that echoed inside me. In a different and in a more lasting way, I have this experience when reading and rereading Simone Weil.

Among the authors who, after opening new paths to my thought, act as a firm point of reference, are also the great names of semiotics, two above all, namely, Charles S. Peirce and Ferdinand de Saussure; actually three, Roman Jakobson as well. Something analogous I should say of Sigmund Freud and of his best disciple, Melanie Klein. And what about those thinkers who have taught me to think better? After completing my education as a student, there remain but a few. There is Aristotle, of course, who guides me even in the negative—but as the genius that he was—in my critique of patriarchy. I entrust "thinking better" mainly to the quality of writing and I learn it by reading, it doesn't matter what. It can be an advertisement slogan or a poetic verse, or the title of a book, such as *Più donne che uomini* (*More Women than Men*) by Ivy Compton-Burnett,[9] who has taught me to say the ways in which sexual difference manifests itself.

In light of this overview, I could be blamed for being affected by Eurocentrism. The overview is incomplete, as one more title is missing, namely, *The Art of War*, a text written by an ancient Chinese teacher of military strategy, Sun Tzu, from whom I have learned something fundamental about authority. On this theme, one can also learn a lot from the novelist Jane Austen . . . And I have come back to my Eurocentrism.

The Eurocentric imprint of my thought cannot be denied and, given my personal history, is inevitable. My readings have expanded to include texts from other cultures, such as Islamic mysticism, but I did not put too much effort in correcting myself by integrating them in the readings of my formation. I have preferred to follow a simpler path, and that is to cultivate a sense of partiality toward Western culture, starting from the awareness of my estrangement as a woman in relation to it.

Precisely for this reason, I am interested in contemporary thinkers who pay attention to the thought of sexual difference. In particular, I have appreciated the essays of the editors of *Another Mother: Diotima and the Symbolic Order of Italian Feminism*, where there is, in closing, a comment to the first chapter about the "Symbolic Order of the Mother," which is much more than a comment, entitled: "Mother Degree Zero; or, of Beginnings."[10]

ER How do you keep "estrangement" and "recollection" together?

LM Recollection has to do with truth and truth . . . I don't know whether we can say truth, but to recognize it, yes, we can. Thus, recollection and estrangement go together in that the estrangement you feel leads you to search for a sense and therefore for truth.

ER You have studied philosophy with Gustavo Bontadini, you have done research and taught at the University of Verona from 1976 to 2006. In a number of your writings, you talk about your conscious choice in becoming a feminist, of having been named a woman, and that this profound change was a turning point for you. Tell us more about this crucial moment in your life, how you came to it and the meaning of this conscious choice for you, both at a personal and at a professional level.

LM Recently, the French newspaper *Le Monde* published a biographical profile of the American economist Deirdre McCloskey, an expert in the history of capitalism. We read that she was male at birth, and she decided to transition later in life but desired to belong to the other sex ever since she was a child: "When I was eleven years old, I cried and prayed God that he would transform me into a girl." These words provide the image that I was looking for in order to speak of my feminist conscious choice in its decisive moment: it happened a little after I was thirty, and it was as if God had granted the eleven-year-old boy's prayer. I experienced a happiness of that type. I, too, was given back to my sexed gender. On paper, I was already female, I was and felt a woman, but a woman who believed that she needed to measure herself against men and their culture if she wanted to become her best self. Around thirty, I started to feel that I was not going to be able to make it because I was emptying myself out of ideas, of the pleasure of working out these ideas in writing.

The decisive moment came when my professor, Gustavo Bontadini, asked me: "Why do you turn to the feminists?" The implication was: there is no reason. "You are *homo*," he added, "nothing more is needed to devote oneself to philosophy." At which, I protested: "But I am a woman." Bontadini asked me to argue my position, but I had no arguments, only the adversative conjunction: "*But* I am a woman." And his question! Before this, I had happened to meet Lia Cigarini, a brilliant feminist from the beginning who had ingenious ideas, and it was because of her that I had "turned to the feminists." She would become my friend for life.

This last fact would be the most important, but certain things, the decisive ones, in order to happen for good, it seems they have to happen twice. When I said that I was a woman and not *homo*, in saying it, I unpinned myself from the neutral and abstract position in which I had placed myself, like an insect for a collection, and where I had believed I should stay in order to speak as a philosopher. To unpin myself and start to think again was one and the same. With this double move I was given back to myself. What does this mean? It means that I was given back to a possibility of being that was not actually there, possible only as a desire and in the form of expectations but that became attainable in the act of realizing that I was that, what was said banally of me, a woman. This accepted coincidence of me with myself has had a tremendous eccentric effect. It threw me out of what I was supposed to be in order to enter philosophy. I was thrown out of myself and I found myself. Where? In my usual body and with my usual name. But in that body, with that same name, I started to really be there, with all—albeit little—the human competence of thinking myself and the world, helped by philosophy and by feminism. Thus, I became what is called a feminist philosopher. I am not a feminine thinking substance! I belong to the great sea of possible being and I have the fortune of having been brought into the world, where I have the possibility—again, the possible—of further becoming myself, thanks to my freedom.

It cannot be excluded a priori that all of this may be instead a misfortune. We are not without reason for thinking this way. I do not think this way because, in the linking up of events that I call the feminist turning point, I have known a definitive burst of happiness.

Since then, I have altered the meaning of the word "contingency" and I have devoted myself to thinking that the contingent being—the non-necessary being—encompasses happy combinations in its constitution. Among these, I count that of being born and being born of the same sex as my mother.

ER You speak of feminism as a double move, a move that at the moment it threw you out and "unpinned" you, at that very moment, it also gave you back to yourself. In other words, the moment you felt outside, you found yourself again, and were able to reconnect with yourself.

LM Exactly. I had taken a place, I thought it was the place I needed to keep, the right place for me, and in that very moment I was thrown out of that place and found myself in the right place. These are things that in telling seem like wonders but they do happen to us human beings because we are symbolic animals, made of body and words. And these are events of a symbolic nature.

ER You just said that in finding feminism you felt a "burst of happiness." Could you describe this happiness?

LM Happiness consists of bursts. For example, when one experiences this coincidence of finding herself, precisely in the moment when she is pulled out, away from where she had taken a place, well, this coincidence is happiness. People know these bursts of happiness when they fall in love, for instance. The sense of happiness eventually fades; we are not able to feel continually happy. However, profound emotions, when paired with intelligence, leave a lasting mark. The thought of the task that I received many years ago still makes me happy today and, at moments, gives me bursts of happiness.

ER One cannot deny that feminism has gone through strong and less strong periods. It has meant a lot for many women, but there are a number of women who not only do not call themselves feminists, they also find the term "feminism" problematic and they dissociate themselves from it, at least here in the US. By way of example, among my young women students, in the course on feminist theory, there are always a few who do not call themselves feminists, even when they are in favor of many policies for women specifically. This happens even in the wake of the Me Too movement that brought everyone's attention, again, to the persistent violence against women, their exploitation by men in positions of power in particular. How do you explain this phenomenon of disconnect between oneself and reality? Is it a lack of awareness? Is it a lack of historical memory and a failure to recognize the battles women have fought? Is the term "feminism" still adequate for today's challenges? How would you define feminism?

LM This question, which is not one question only, but many, concerns the theme of the transmission of thought among individuals, cultures, and generations. This topic is nothing new but becomes new when it is about women among themselves, between you and your young women students, in this case. In the past, women who enjoyed a certain authority—such as mothers, schoolteachers, the women superiors in religious communities—were in charge of transmitting the law of the father—in the family—and of man—in society—with the additional duty of attesting to it in the cultures into which they might have migrated. I have seen that myself while visiting an Italian immigrant community in Belgium.

Things have changed a great deal, and it would take too long to explain why and how. Feminism has something to do with it, and here I begin. Today I am asked a question by a feminist professor on the transmission of feminist thought in this way: "Among my students, there are always a few who do not call themselves feminists."

A woman I know very well and who has supported me in my choices, my older sister, does not consider herself a feminist. I think I know why. In her life and in her vision of the world, there are choices, thoughts, and, perhaps, also desires that do not agree with feminism as it has been understood up to now: perhaps in the future? A feminism that is in contrast with the experience of a woman on an important point is missing something, I would think.

By this example I want to say that a young woman may be aspiring to something that is not there in what she has taken feminism to be. Her contrariety is a signal that she sends you. That is all. It is here that you matter as a teacher.

Incidentally, let me just say that an academic subject such as feminist theory risks being a push that forces you to think that certain things are true in themselves and for themselves. If this were the case, the student in question would be right. If, on the other hand, you teach knowing that the subjective truth cannot be skipped, then the problem is another—it is a problem of authority in your relationship between you who teach and the student who learns. A female student who does not wish to waste time, money, and energy will listen to you with the trust needed to measure your teaching on her experience and to reflect upon that personally. You must demand this authority, not as a prerogative but as a quality of your relationship, which is as indispensable to her as it is to you.

What do I mean by "subjective truth"? Indicatively, I mean that you are present in what you say as a witness and a guarantor so that you would not say it if you did not think it true. Without this presence of yourself in what you affirm—what I call subjective truth—the highly praised objectivity would make us speak according to the dominant symbolic order and would be the "truth of the regime." Michel Foucault, in *Les mots et les choses* (*The Order of Things*),[11] has opened our eyes to the production of truth by the dominant discursive regime. But he did not think of what the feminist movement would discover in those years, namely, that there are political practices in which it is possible to speak from the position of symbolic independence from power: practices in which it is possible to generate what is true.

ER Beyond your critique of me as a teacher—something that would require looking into the specific situation—in what you say I hear, implicitly, the question of the translatability of feminism into an academic context.

LM About the critique, I admit that I do not know the specific context of what you have evoked. I always try to teach, even to women professors; it is something stronger than myself. What I mean to say is that searching for what is true and just can be done and turning it into something to be taught is an entirely different thing. That is to say, feminism as theoretical research can be done, but that in itself is not the same as the subjective choice.

ER There is thus a difference between the subjective experience of feminism and feminism as a theoretical knowledge, meaning that feminism is not so much a theory but a practice or practices, which cannot be reduced to theory only.

LM About this I am reminded of what Lia Cigarini says—she is the one who introduced me to feminist thought and she is still an authority for me. She asks: "What is theory?" and she answers: "It is practice put into words." She sees clearly on this. I do not. I know that theory is necessary, and I also know that theory is not enough. If we say it with Hannah Arendt, if we think that we can replace experience or reality with some theoretical view, then we fall into error. As a matter of fact, sometimes I counterpose theory to story; at times it is the practice, but at times it is the story, namely, to say the story of the things that happen. It is also true that I have an aptitude for theory, I have been formed by theory, and I think that theory—thinking and reasoning theoretically—is indispensable. But it is not necessary that everyone engages in it. Instead, it is necessary that reasoning thought does not pretend to complete the discourse and that it leaves room for experience.

ER Some thinkers, I think for instance of bell hooks, an African American feminist thinker, speaks of theory as a form of "healing," that is, a form of care that helps heal the wounds and the pain one has suffered.

LM It is a very interesting view. It is understanding theory as a way of putting things in order, a symbolic order, and thereby being able to say those things that, when she experienced them, did not have this meaning or did not allow her to see it. Yes, I find that to be very interesting.

ER Going back to practice: it would seem that a choice of awareness, a reflection on oneself, is necessary.

LM Many years ago, I gave a course on practice. It was not an academic course, even though it happened at a university. Practice is a great philosophical theme, especially in Italian philosophy. One could think of Gramsci, Vico, or Machiavelli. The theory of practice is thought, but what is it? For the women's movement, what has practice been? It has been a way of creating situations that would free thought. The first practice was that of *autocoscienza*—consciousness raising—that is, to gather in private homes and speak of our lived experiences, say those thoughts that we thought were not worthy of being said. In my philosophical vocation, I discovered that there were thoughts that were not worthy of words. In those gatherings, we told each other things we had kept inside, lived things, things we remembered, and we told them among friends until four in the morning. We created a situation in which it became possible to voice thoughts we thought unworthy of being said, an example given to us by American women. Through this we discovered many things, for instance, that starting from oneself was what we had in common with other women and that our experiences were shared by other women. Practice was what we were doing. It was a free course that was not in the programs, that did not have a fixed place—with the help of janitors we would find an open room—and, for two or three hours, we would sit there talking about what practice is. I was inspired by my experience of feminism, which I found excellent.

Another example is the Diotima community at the University of Verona,[12] where the main seminar is open to the public; we have gatherings with male colleagues and students, yet Diotima does philosophical research only among women. This is a choice of practice. Practice, thus, is about arranging things, it is to put things together. Things are contrived either by tradition and power or because someone says, "This is how we do it," and this imposition counts a lot: how to proceed, at what time and in what place, whom to address, whom not to address, and so on. All of this counts a great deal. Therefore, it counts a lot to do it by free choice in order to help one's own personal capacity for understanding, for opening up and for changing oneself.

ER It would seem that the academic system does not lend itself to this kind of practice.

LM The "system" doesn't, but new situations can be invented even from within academic contexts. There are freedoms that can be taken without doing violence. At the time it was possible to do so. These are freedoms that one needs to take, and this can be done without violence. There are margins, which maybe we don't even see, where it is possible to do things freely. At the time, there were more margins that were left empty, free, not thought. Now, there is a society that is more organized, to the smallest details, and maybe there are less margins.

I'll give you another example. When I taught at the *istituto magistrale*[13] in Rovereto, near Trento—I have taught at all school levels—there were some female students who said that bars scared them and made them feel ashamed. I, on the other hand, am used to going to a bar to read or for a coffee as we do in Italy. So, one day, without asking permission of the principal, I took my students to a bar. Let's go to a bar and see what happens. These were teenage girls and some had had traumatic experiences; for example, one had forced herself to go to a bar alone and, in entering the bar, she fell down. The principal complained, she gave me an earful, but I did not care. She had the power and had to show it. But these are the margins I am talking about. There are more margins than we realize, and we must take them. Surely, it takes a certain kind of temperament. I was a rebel, reasonable and clever, but not for the sake of provocation. With my mother, too, I always did what I wanted to do; now and then, we would clash and even though she got angry at me, she understood me very well; she was like me or, better, I was like her. With such a temperament, and without doing any violence, but by embracing freedom, which is an inspiration for the individual woman, I did a lot. This is there for everyone, but then there is the particular case for every person.

When I see relationships becoming dependent on me, it is trying for me, I have a hard time accepting that. Symbolic independence is not just a stance, a turning point. Certainly, it is this—I was talking earlier about the *autocoscienza* groups in feminism, which have been moments of symbolic independence—but it is also something that needs to be cultivated in oneself. I used to think that dependence was bad. After trying everything I could to free myself from dependence, I have understood that it should not be transformed into something bad, that it can be lived because it reveals a condition that is structured within the human condition: to live with others' dependence. However, when it becomes a burden and something that holds one back inside, it is tiring and it can be heavy, humiliating, both in living it and in causing it. It must be taken in this light: dependence on others is there, but there is also freedom, there is a call, there is duty, and there is being free. Marguerite says of freedom: "the gift that God never takes back."

ER You are known in Italy and abroad as one of the central figures, if not the central figure, of the thought of sexual difference. Many of your works talk about the thought of sexual difference, as their titles attest: *Diotima: Il pensiero della differenza sessuale, Tre lezioni sulla differenza sessuale e altri scritti*. Other works talk about it indirectly, such as the *L'ordine simbolico della madre, Diotima: Oltre l'eguaglianza: Le radici femminili dell'autorità*,[14] just to name a few. To think of Luisa Muraro means, at the same time, to think of the thought of sexual difference or, in other words, we cannot think of the thought of sexual difference without thinking of Luisa Muraro. Could you say why such a strong connection exists, this intertwining between Luisa Muraro and the thought of sexual difference? What does this connection between yourself as a woman and the thought of sexual difference express?

LM What you say about the deep connection between the so-called thought of sexual difference and myself corresponds to me: I feel it, other women say it. The formula, however, goes back to Luce Irigaray, who remains the most authoritative thinker of this thought. It was picked up by me in an interview with Luisa Cavaliere for the newspaper *l'Unità* and it imposed itself as the first title of the book published by Diotima, a title that was suggested by Adriana Cavarero who, at the time, was part of our philosophical community.

Why would there be such a deep intertwining between me and the thought of sexual difference? I believe I know. In my childhood, I have always mulled over what was happening around me. But years later, I did not feel attracted to philosophy any longer. The choice of philosophical studies had been suggested by those who had offered me a university scholarship. Bontadini, my professor of reference, had, in turn, ancient metaphysics—Aristotle and Parmenides—as his point of reference. One day, he asked me why I was not actively participating in his seminar, although I attended it regularly. "Metaphysics does not attract me," I answered. "Why do you attend it then?" "Because the philosophy of those who do not measure themselves up with metaphysics is poor." The professor seemed happy about my answer, and it was he who, later, would open the doors to philosophy for me by calling me *homo*. I woke up to the philosophical thought in the act in which the fact of sexual difference imposed itself to me and led me to answer, "But I am a woman!" I was not proclaiming an essence, I was naming a contingent fact—it so just happens that I am a woman—but, for me, it was an inescapable fact in which contingence and necessity were confused until it became, thanks to feminism, an accepted fact. In this way, I reconnected with the thinker that I was as a child, when I lived in society with my sisters and my brothers, before I began to attend school.

The most notable thing, perhaps, is that nothing was lost of what I learned at school; *everything* turned out to be useful. Thus, I place sexual difference on the side of the subject, and when the context allows it, I prefer to say "the thinking sexual difference." Everything, even metaphysics? Yes, it has taught me the language of partiality and of plurality that does not end up with relativism, the language of conjecture (*conjectura*) in the meaning it has in Nicholas of Cusa.

ER You just referred to Luce Irigaray, a philosopher and a psychoanalyst, a thinker who is very important for your thought. You are the translator of many of her books into Italian, for example, *Speculum: L'altra donna* (*Speculum: Of the Other Woman*), *Questo sesso che non è un sesso* (*This Sex Which Is Not One*),[15] and others. Undoubtedly, Irigaray has exercised a great influence on your work and on the thought of sexual difference in Italy, a thought that has its own specific features. Tell us about this influence and its relevance for you as a woman and for the thought of sexual difference in Italy. What are the most salient points in this relationship? Has this relationship changed over time and, if so, how?

LM The feminism that I have come to know in Italy, in the 1970s, was part of an international movement and was nourished by ideas coming from different countries, Italy included. In 1970, the *Manifesto di Rivolta Femminile*, followed by other writings by Carla Lonzi that we still read today, began to circulate. In 1969, the DEMAU group published *Il maschile come valore dominante* (Maleness as the dominant value). In Lonzi's work, what stands out is the irreducible difference—"alterity"—between woman and man; in the work by the DEMAU group, we find delineated the idea of the politics of the symbolic. Both texts reject the feminist ideal of equality.[16]

Speculum: De l'autre femme by Luce Irigaray was published in 1974 in France and a year later in Italy, where it found fertile ground, and the book saw a great and lasting success, just as her subsequent books had. The last book of Irigaray that I translated came out in 1987, *Sexes et parentés* (*Sexes and Genealogies*).[17] My relationship of collaboration with her lasted until the early 1990s. By translating her work and by being her interpreter at public events for a number of years, I had the double fortune of assimilating her thought and of participating in expanding the women's movement. When I am asked about my relationship with Luce Irigaray, this is the answer I give: I did not read Irigaray, I *translated* her, in the etymological sense of the word "translate," that is, to make her pass through me in order to bring her to other women. I have never separated the contributions of Luce Irigaray from the contributions of other feminists, including the anonymous ones who rushed to listen to her, because all were an active part of a sociality that had not been seen before, and all made possible the feminine activism that has changed the old society. It is in this context that my vocation as a feminist thinker has matured.

To Luce Irigaray, personally, I owe the example of her nobility in approaching and discussing the great themes of philosophy. I know I owe a great debt to her, so great that I cannot measure it. I distanced myself from her when she started to propose objective means in order to realize a feminine culture, such as inscribing positive rights appropriate for women by means of legislation.

ER This distancing from Luce Irigaray, can it be traced back to a particular moment?

LM It doesn't seem right to me to speak of a distancing even though I no longer read what she writes, except for her articles that appear in Italian newspapers. She always says profound things. In the 1970s, I found myself participating in the expansion of feminism in Italy and, at the same time, I was translating Irigaray's books and was able to learn from her thought. An extraordinary good fortune. From her, I have learned to give myself authority in the interpretation of philosophical authors and texts.

ER Specifically, with regard to the thought of sexual difference in Italy, as one of the prominent voices, how would you describe it to someone who, from outside the Italian context, is not very familiar with it? What are its main theoretical tenets and how do they manifest themselves in practice? How is it different from the thought of sexual difference in France?

LM Years ago, I published a book, *Maglia o uncinetto*,[18] aiming at showing how context contributes to the meaning of what we say, even the non-linguistic context. The science of language distinguishes pragmatics from semantics with the criterion of taking or not taking into consideration the context of linguistic communication, but this does not mean that not taking the context into consideration can be truly done in communicating with others.

This is to say that I do not have a thought of sexual difference that I can present outside my context. It is not an object of theoretical thought; it is a subjective thought, endowed with subjective truth. It does not have the fact of being sexed as its object—being born male or female by reproduction from two different individuals—but its meaning, the meaning that it takes for us humans to be born with a sex that makes us different, due to which we call ourselves women/men. The difference is not *between*, but *in*: between a man and a woman the differences are countless and various, like all individual differences; sexual difference, by contrast, inheres in me, is internal to me and, at the same time, is felt as a lack, a differing of myself from myself. I can give importance to this sentiment or ignore it. But, as I have said, when I put it into words, I became aware of myself and began to think. An inner and free coincidence took place.

To me, the thought of sexual difference resembles a story more than a theory; in feminism there are countless events and therefore many tales that tell a story that tends to coincide with the historical meaning, which is the breaking down of masculine dominance once confronted with the feminine demand for freedom.

The feminism of difference seeks a free sense of sexual difference, starting from women's desire for freedom. To ignore the fact of being sexed or denying its historicity does not do away with the contradictions and the conflicts within the human condition due to the fact of being sexed, which cannot be reduced to a historical product but in itself produces history, as Geneviève Fraisse teaches us in *La sexuation du monde: Réflexions sur l'émancipation*.[19] This means that we need to take up again the negotiation with our being a female body, even in the absence of masculine discrimination. There is no *happy end* to the question of difference, and fortunately we must say because the scientific thought of a separation between biology and psychology is not there—as we saw with semiotics and pragmatics. There is no clear-cut division between biology and psychology, between the symbolic and the social . . . and there is no end to the subjective search for a free sense of sexual difference.

One of my female students told us that, one day, upon returning home earlier than usual, she found her younger brother dressed up with her clothes and with her makeup on, admiring himself in the mirror. She was stunned and he fled. What was this young boy looking for in his sister's room? He was an explorer looking for something other in order to find himself.

ER A central point in the thought of sexual difference is that it does not support a politics of emancipation founded on the equality between man and woman but practices instead a politics grounded in sexual difference. For those who are not familiar with the thought of sexual difference, this may appear like a position that goes backward rather than moving forward. Please, explain the reasons for such a position.

LM In the way this question has been framed there lies, in my view, an error of interpretation that concerns the second wave of feminism, namely, the resurgence of feminism at the end of the 1960s. The question implies that feminism overall was moved by a desire of emancipation, with the exception of the feminism of difference. That is not the case. The feminism of difference is a name coined later in order to differentiate ourselves from those feminists who, in the name of the ideal of equality, endorsed a politics of equality between man and woman.

A correct reading of the facts shows that yes, in the feminine society, there was a widespread expectation of emancipation. In the countries at an advanced stage of capitalism, this expectation was met with an offer of feminine emancipation—integration and equality with men. But, precisely in these countries, the creation of small groups of *autocoscienza*—consciousness raising—which were separate from men, stepped in as a real break with regard to this regular and anticipated progress. Most people have not understood this; it was in fact the direct answer to ignored suffering. The suffering of emancipation is the countermelody to the career of Marilyn Monroe, by way of example, which was heard and found reparation in the Me Too movement. About this last event, the aspect of revolt against sexist violence has been greatly emphasized, and not enough has been said of the disrupting aspect of an agreement among some women for public denunciation not directed at the law first and foremost. Many centuries since Marguerite Porete wrote the *Mirror of Simple Souls*, her program is taken up again where she, her protagonist, the free soul, "is above the law, not against the law."

At the beginning, the separate group involved a few women, in the US as elsewhere, but their example is contagious and ends up transforming even the widespread demand for emancipation, which becomes a revolt against sexism and a search for freedom thanks to an altered relationship among women.

The final objection regarding the question that charges the feminism of difference of moving backward simply picks up again an objection that was made by second wave feminism, by emancipated women who interpreted the choice of separation from male society as a retreat: they could not see its profound significance. Later, this objection faded but, within feminism, a differentiation began to be made between a fair feminism that is acceptable and a "radical" feminism. Through a label, a rather complex and historical reality in becoming was thus simplified.

If we do not accept the solution provided by labels, the question becomes: How has the confrontation between the two feminisms ended? It has ended in that from two they have become many. Actually though, the confrontation between the initial break and "normality" is not over, and the Me Too movement proves it. The confrontation has spread from small groups into the wide world and continues to renew itself, in the feminist movement as well as in politics and in society. The initial break has become a historical turning point and is part of the contemporary world's unrest.

ER The question contains an error of interpretation in the sense that the perception of feminine difference as a dimension of the human and not complementary to man is there from the beginnings of feminism in the late 1960s and early 1970s and it is not a later development, is that it?

LM Precisely. The irreversible leap of the wave of feminism of the 1970s in Italy—1960s in America—was the sense of difference, not emancipation. The feminism of symbolic independence has convinced many women, who did not call themselves feminists, to become feminists.

ER One main criticism of the thought of sexual difference, especially of Irigaray's thought of sexual difference, is that it is essentialist. As far as the thought of sexual difference in Italy is concerned, do you find that it is a valid criticism? Why? Why not? How would you respond to this criticism?

LM The pair essentialism/existentialism establishes an opposition that has not given rise to significant developments.

Another thing is the case of the critique of essentialism that some women, within feminism, move toward the feminism of difference. This critique signals a difficulty of interpretation with regard to sexual difference, a difficulty that endures because it arises out of the insurmountable ambiguity of our being/having a body. What is the significance of sexual difference? Does it enable me to be who I am and therefore I have to integrate it into myself—as the language I speak suggests with the feminine/masculine grammatical genders? Or do I confine it to the body, to the biological sphere? Or must the answer be sought in the contingent social forms that have made me an emancipated woman, in the same way as in different contexts, they would have subjugated me or something else, depending? The difficulty becomes even more complicated because of the different relation that we have, males and females, men and women, with our respective bodies due to the asymmetry in procreation.

In the past, up to our day, we have dealt with this further difficulty by way of a hierarchic relation that has subordinated motherhood to fatherhood. The hierarchic response does not hold any more, but the alternative of equality is not viable either—equality is a mirage—and gives rise to an asymmetric difference that defies the modern principle of equality. It defies it, it does not deny it, from whence the politics of equal opportunity, for instance.

In my judgment, these are real difficulties. The thought of sexual difference is a challenge to political practice and to philosophical thought. Rightly so, Luce Irigaray has posed sexual difference as the issue to be thought in our age.

ER Could you elaborate further on the ambiguity of our being body?

LM We tend to reduce our being body to having a body, but are we body or do we have a body? The ambiguity is found right in there, in being a body and in having a body. The more powerful the technology, the more it seems it replaces our being body. For example, female bodies are able to reproduce; male bodies are not, even though they provide an indispensable contribution. There is the technological temptation to make the male body able to reproduce, a temptation that has always been there. Our bodies are sexed, but sexual difference is in culture, in psychology, and in biology.

ER You just said that the thought of sexual difference is a challenge to political practice and to philosophy, and you juxtaposed it to the "mirage of equality."

LM It is a challenge because the peculiar role of women in procreation introduces an asymmetry in the thinking subject. Aristotle turned the asymmetry of the two sexes' contribution upside down, giving the male the role of the parent in the sense of generating life. Since then, the male has been considered the superior sex, until science was able to demonstrate the fallacy of Aristotle's theory.

It is a challenge because biological sex is an invention of evolutionary life and does not obey a physical law such as the law of gravity, without exception. Bodies of uncertain sexual identity are born and there are human beings that do not accept their own biological sex. There is no determinism between anatomy and human identity. This is why I told the story of my friend who, coming home, found her brother in her room with her clothes on; he, male, was investigating what one feels like being female. Transness is not a disease; it is an adventure of the human, especially in the form of being born male—still a privilege to this day—and desiring to be female. It is a question of extraordinary complexity, and it must be thought through.

ER Are you saying that the critique of essentialism tends to flatten, simplify the complexity of sexual difference?

LM Yes, but the critique of essentialism must be taken seriously and confronted in the first person, as males and females. We do not belong entirely to one sex or another; we belong to humanity, and humanity is sexed. We accept and, at the same time, we become who we are, enriching ourselves in the relationship of difference and exchange with what we are not, and opposing the sexual roles that we find unjust and unacceptable.

ER Within the Italian context, the thought of sexual difference is very strong, but there are other feminist stances. How does the thought of sexual difference distinguish itself from these other positions? How do you see the relation between the thought of sexual difference and other ways of understanding, being, and practicing feminism? Do you agree with characterizing feminism in the plural or not? Why?

LM The mediocrity with which some publications seek to illustrate various feminisms makes me prefer the use of the word in the singular. It is a preference, nothing more. In the past, I did not like the word in the singular either. Now, I accept it, I say I am feminist: have I changed or has the linguistic use changed? Most likely, both.

I do not have the necessary preparation to give an honest view on Italian feminism overall. I would have to decide how to distinguish the Italian context from other contexts, a thing that I don't think I can do, and then, I would have to distinguish the thought of sexual difference from other theoretical positions, something I prefer not to do. Instead, I'd rather let these differences within the women's movement continue to talk among themselves, even if in conflict. In this plurality of voices, it is the *differences among women* that speak and these differences among women are the only portrayal that I can draw about feminine difference without falling into stereotypes.

ER Why is feminism in the singular alright but not "feminisms" in the plural?

LM Because it does not resolve anything. Feminism is a battlefield. We can speak of feminisms in the plural but, at the end, the issue is always about fighting the sexist domination, the subordination of the feminine to the masculine. From the very start, the feminism of the 1970s in Italy was this: we understood that emancipation was not enough, that, as women, we were different, and that sexual difference needed to be reevaluated. We did not fight for equality, which was a way of honoring the masculine sex and wanting to be like them.

ER In listening to what you just said, Hannah Arendt's concepts of uniqueness, distinction, and plurality come to mind, even though she does not speak of sexual difference.

LM Hannah Arendt does not speak of sexual difference and cannot be considered feminist, but she has been adopted by feminist thought for her peculiar brilliance, as is the case with Simone Weil. In the twentieth century, both are teachers of thought. There are feminist thinkers, such as Adriana Cavarero, who give Arendt the merit of having recognized the value of birth and having given us a philosophy of natality.

ER In the last decades, in the context of the US, there has been a growing social recognition of homosexuality, lesbianism, and other forms of sexuality that do not conform to the traditional model of heterosexuality. LGBTQ+—lesbian, gay, bisexual, transgendered, queer—is a movement, in its various forms, that keeps fighting for inclusion, challenging the idea of heterosexuality as a norm and that there are only two sexes. The thought of sexual difference starts with the affirmation that there are two sexes and thereby it would appear to side with the heterosexual matrix, against the claims of LGBTQ+. Is it so? What is the position of the thought of sexual difference in this regard?

LM The movement that gathers the various "sexual minorities" in defense of their dignity and rights has also existed in Italy for some time. Obviously, not all the people indicated in the acronym associate themselves with the movement. On the contrary, some dissent openly, among them a portion of lesbians who claim to be women and feminists, first of all.

As far as I am concerned, for a time now, I have lost the interest I used to have initially for this movement, an interest motivated by a theme I thought we shared, the search for a free sense of sexual difference. I have lost this interest for two reasons that amount to one: the indifference to sexual difference. This probably reflects the movement's masculine hegemony.

The free sense of sexual difference is understood as "whatever you want," with a laissez-faire interpretation of freedom: absence of necessity. And the difference becomes a diversity, misunderstanding the very principle of being sexed, which confronts us, as all animals, with the necessary heterosexual procreation.

I observe, incidentally, that the latter distortion, by way of which "difference" becomes "diversity," recurs frequently in the masculine language, for example in the Italian translation of Evelyn Fox Keller's book *Sul genere e la scienza* (*Reflections on Gender and Science*),[20] where *differenza*—difference—is systematically translated as *diversità*—diversity.

Besides, the feminist aspiration has been lost to a generically progressive aspiration, aimed at the realization of new rights or pseudo-rights such as those of becoming fathers of creatures bought at the market of surrogate mothers—or *gpa gravidanza per altri*, "pregnancy for others" in English. This "progressive" movement seeks to affirm itself in the institutions, but it also seeks the support of the women's movement. I must say that it has obtained fair support from feminism, though I am not in a position to quantify it. It is a controversial issue, but it does not appear to me that it is about the issue of hetero/homosexuality. The controversy is mostly about the biological necessity of heterosexual procreation and the various attempts at overcoming it, and overcoming the primary significance of the maternal relationship.

ER Difference is not *diversity* (*diversità*).

LM Not at all to my ear and not in English nor in Italian, but . . . There is a problem: the pair difference/diversity is much more significant in philosophy than in everyday language. It is not simply a nuance. Everything that is not identical is diverse. Difference, on the other hand, has a more specific sense: in what is different, something has happened for which there is no identity, it is not just something whatever but determined, actually determining. What has happened with sexual difference? What has happened is the fact of being sexed, so that life is reproduced between two living beings of the same species, but different. It would be necessary here to dwell on how the human species has accounted for sexual difference through language and through culture and how it affects the conscious awareness of the individual person. In this conversation, I have given the example of my coming to conscious awareness of my sexual difference.

ER Staying with the issue of sexual minorities, could you say more about your position?

LM Maybe I am not the best person to answer this question. Militants of the LGBTQ+ movement fight for their rights and inclusion on par, something that is more fitting with the USA, which, as a nation, was born at the time of the Universal Declaration of Human Rights and is afflicted with racism and other forms of marginalization. This is not the case in Italy, an old country, where the acquisition of rights has been important but not fundamental. In Italy, the free sense of difference, against privileges, against hierarchies, against affiliations, and against conformity counts more. What counts is gaining symbolic independence against subservience and the tendency to imitate.

ER Judith Butler, a well-known and respected thinker, thinks that the heterosexual matrix is an ideological device that reduces and imposes just two sexes, the male and the female, condemning those who do not identify with either to a condition of exclusion and marginality, even of violence.

LM Human dignity does not begin with rights but with freedom, and with the interrogation of the possible free sense of what is not free, such as being born and dying. Being sexed belongs to this order of reality, one that precedes being human but that the human being cannot ignore; as a matter of fact, it is registered in customs and traditions—the heterosexual marriage among them—in identities of sexual minorities, in language with different grammatical genders, as well as in psychology. This type of interrogation is of profound significance and demands to be regulated by way of rights. But it cannot be resolved once and for all, and, perhaps, it cannot be resolved at all. Still, it continues to engender culture.

ER Your work comes out of the political practice of feminism at the end of the 1960s and the beginning of the 1970s, a political practice that begins with the separation from men on the part of women. Women leave and they begin their groups of *autocoscienza*—consciousness raising—out of which the Milan Women's Bookstore was born, a place that has played a central role in Italian feminism and is also the epicenter of the thought of sexual difference in Italy. Does this characterization in broad strokes correspond to your experience? Could you expand on the significance of this act of separation from official politics, for women's politics?

LM In this story that you summarize, the central passage has been that of changing not *the world*, as the '68 revolt aspired to do, *not ourselves* in order to adapt to society as they had taught us to do, but the relationship *between ourselves and the world*.

We have even spoken of a "revolt within the revolt," the revolt of women against the 1968 revolt, or the refusal of emancipation, namely, the refusal of the perspective of integration into the male society that was gradually opening to us, daughters of middle-class families. At the beginning we were few, but we became more and more every day. We specified that, in order to change our relationship with the world, it would have been decisive to find and prefer feminine mediations: between the world and me, another woman, we used to say. This led us to prefer the project of creating together a bookstore where we would sell books written by women. An expert we consulted told us: "It will not work" and added "but . . . ," and as a matter of fact it worked very well. The various expressions I have used—"change our relationship with the world," "the revolt within the revolt," "refusal of emancipation"—explain, in different ways, the break with the movement and the groups of 1968. But they say more, they let us intuit the secret of the long duration of the women's movement that started at the end of the 1960s. In short, in a world that was becoming global, that is to say, no longer a world, no longer a history, the withdrawal from a collective engagement to change the world has meant an opening toward the unexpected. As Massimo De Carolis, an acute observer, has written,[21] separating a space with high symbolic value from the rest of the world—and the women's groups of *autocoscienza* were this—that is to say, the act of "dissociating" from the real does not necessarily amount to an escape from reality and can, on the contrary, open a breach in the realization of the unthought.

The task is that of moving in this position of openness, of opening passageways in the identitarian enclosures. It is not easy, and I know this from my experience with the Women's Bookstore. Françoise Collin has admirably described this approach in an essay devoted to the crisis of modernity. Feminism is untranslatable in modern political terms even though it cannot help trying to do so. She then goes on to say that when it is articulated in specific objectives, point by point, feminism is both translated and betrayed at the same time. On the one hand, there is no political gain that does not involve the risk of swinging back against women; on the other, there is no political project that can assume the feminist demand (*esigenza*). She concludes by saying that, for feminism, it is a risk to entrust itself to politics as much as it is resisting going with it.[22] Françoise Collin too expresses herself through paradoxes. Is it realistic to propose staying in this position? Yes and no. The paradox lies in the idea of women's politics itself: feminists cannot form a party, not even when they have positions that are clearly partial, because women are a part that stands for the whole.

ER Here we go back to the question of feminism as a practice that does not let itself be translated easily, or completely, into theory.

LM I mean to say that feminism cannot overlook politics, but that it cannot be completely translated into politics for its own sake, as Françoise Collin says. Her writing entrusts itself to paradoxes and I see myself in that.

ER But it does not seem to leave much possibility: to go through politics is problematic; not to go through politics is also problematic.

LM Yes, as a matter of fact, sexual difference has not been created in order to be resolved. It is a complication of life—of the living being—in order to make it more fascinating, more varied, and more complex. If we were just sexless microbes, all the same, it would amount to nothing. Animals are sexed, but they do not speak or make works of art about this in the way that human beings do. Sexual difference is in the midst of what is human. It is not about resolving it but about complicating existence and making it more varied and fascinating. I like that it is so.

ER Earlier you said that feminism does not have a "happy end."

LM No. It does not.

ER Going back to what you said just before, women are a part that stands for the whole. Could you say more?

LM It is a figurative way of speaking to mean that a woman gives birth to man as well. Simple? Not as it seems, especially for men.

ER *Non credere di avere dei diritti* (*Sexual Difference: A Theory of Social-Symbolic Practice*)[23] is an important book for the women's movement in Italy: it provides an account of women's political practice in the late 1960s and the 1970s. On the back cover of the Italian edition, we read that the theme of the book is "the creation of a feminine genealogy." In the introduction there is discussion of the necessity of a feminine symbolic placement that has been named the "practice of entrustment" (*pratica dell'affidamento*), described as the entrusting of a woman to another woman. It is precisely this "mediation" that gives a foundation to feminine freedom and makes it present in the world. Thus, "feminine genealogy," "practice of entrustment," "mediation," and "feminine freedom" are tied together and they make manifest an interdependence between freedom and relationships among women. Can you tell us more about the relationship between feminine freedom and relationships among women, and how this is crucial for a feminine symbolic?

LM The Italian peninsula has a very long history and the struggle for feminine freedom does not begin with the acquisition of rights. It begins with friendships among women. Not even the history of democracy in Italy begins with rights, but with the struggle for social justice. This must be said so that we can defend ourselves from the dominant narrative. And it is good that some, in the USA, have coined the formula "Italian Difference" with reference also to the feminist ideas.

The title of the book that tells the story of the first years of the Milan Women's Bookstore, between 1975 and 1986, is taken from the *Cahiers* of Simone Weil, a countercurrent French philosopher who, in Italy, has many passionate readers, men and women. Feminism has adopted her. In your summary, the connection between the gain in freedom and the relationships among women is presented as a chapter of a theory, but originally it was a discovery acquired through practice. *Non credere di avere dei diritti* (*Sexual*

Difference: A Theory of Social-Symbolic Practice) is a story accompanied by our interpretation, that is, the interpretation by we who are also involved. What is a theory? A practice put into words, says the most authoritative among us, a practice that engenders others. Many are in fact the practices that, step by step, intertwine with our experiences, that become increasingly more complex because of social changes.

When the French Revolution ideas of equality and freedom founded on the law imposed themselves all over Europe, they spoke of universal rights, yet they did not apply to women. They would be extended to women later and the most blatant discriminations would be removed from legal codes, although they tend to endure in society. It is women who, as they became more conscious, fought those discriminations not so much because they are discriminations but for themselves and for their daughters. This is how history has gone if it is read from below and not from the official point of view.

The expansion of feminism in Italy did not slow down, not even in the 1980s, when movements and parties on the left were in crisis. These are the years when capitalism prevailed over the Communist Block. The international women's movement was also affected by this, but not in Italy: Why? Because we did not claim our rights; instead, we invented the political practice that turned out to be most effective: that of recognizing and empowering the relationships among women. This is the meaning of the title of the story of the Milan Women's Bookstore: not the search for an equality consistent with the law, but the search for a symbolic independence from a law that is patriarchal in its origins. This is also true for other groups in Italy and outside Italy. I do not dare to say for feminism as a whole, even though I think so and I see that this approach is shared by an increasing number of men.

ER This practice of relationships among women differs from the politics of rights, seeks the symbolic independence from patriarchy, and does not pursue equality. In what way does it empower women and make them feel authoritative?

LM In the background is the mother figure, who is a fearsome figure both for women and for men; but she is also a source of symbolic force, and a source of authority. Feminism has also recognized sisterhood, or friendship between women, or love between women, in lesbianism above all. Thus, there are various modalities of relationships among women and the type of relationship one has had with her mother influences these relationships as well. I would not be able to reduce all these various modalities of relationship to one type alone. I say only that it has been a great discovery: that the world we partake in is populated by women, by more and more women, and that some of them are very funny, very skilled, very intelligent, and very beautiful. One develops feelings for women, not necessarily sexual feelings, and this comes back to empower oneself. When women are on the sexual market there is rivalry, but if women meet among themselves, speak to one another, without rivalry, they are empowering themselves. This is not to say that there are no problems; women are not all the same and all equally endowed with intelligence, skills, and so on.

When we discovered the alliance among women as our political goal, we felt this sentiment of alliance strongly, without resentment toward men, without even wanting to go against them, and it has worked.

This is shared by an increasing number of men who do not reason only in terms of rights, but who recognize the excellence of being woman that is an excellence that precedes the equality of rights.

ER The recognition of feminine authority hinges on the recognition of disparity among women, namely, that women are not all alike, that there exist differences among them and that some women are more authoritative than others. The recognition that there exist women who exercise their authority and become points of reference for other women is a cornerstone of the thought of sexual difference as practiced in Italy. Please explain the significance of this "discovery" and how politics becomes work on the symbolic.

LM The proposal of distinguishing authority from power and developing a sense of authority in politics makes its way in Italian feminism at the end of the 1980s and affirms itself with important contributions in the 1990s. Among them is the excellent book by Diotima, *Oltre l'uguaglianza*[24] (Beyond equality).

The topic arose after the very serious accident at the Chernobyl thermonuclear power plant in Ukraine—at the time part of the Soviet Union—in the spring of 1986. The first text does not name authority explicitly, but it is essentially all about that. It is Lia Cigarini's "Prendere scienza e forza da una fonte femminile" (Taking science and force from a feminine source),[25] which first appeared in *Quaderni di donne e politica*, as part of the proceedings of the conference Scienza, potere, coscienza del limite: Dopo Chernobyl—oltre l'estraneità (Science, power, awareness of a limit: After Chernobyl—beyond estrangement). These titles speak for themselves as they name the contradiction between feminism and politics. The theme of authority, feminine authority in the first place, becomes more precise and stronger at the intersection between critique of politics, on the one hand, and empowering women's politics, on the other. Some of us, the older ones, came out of the anti-authoritarian movement and we were listened to on this subject.

In 1991, a revised and expanded version of "What Is Authority?" by Hannah Arendt was published in Italian and it confirmed the necessary distinction between authority and power, encouraging us to carry on. One needed and needs courage in a culture that systematically confuses authority and power.

It must be said that we already had some pretty good ideas derived from our political practice. Among these was the refusal of the equality man–woman as a political goal. We identified with the words by Mary Catherine Bateson: "To different degrees, each of the five of us has been discriminated against because we are women; we have all sometimes been treated as less than equal. But each of us seeks out relationships of difference, a little puzzled by the necessary political thrust toward equality. Unless we treasure our differences, we will never achieve interdependence." (*In misura diversa ciascuna di noi ha subito discriminazioni per il fatto di essere donna; tutte siamo state qualche volta trattate come meno uguali. Ma tutte siamo sempre alla ricerca di rapporti di differenza, un po' disorientate dalla necessaria accettazione politica dell'uguaglianza. A meno di fare tesoro delle nostre differenze, non conquisteremo mai l'interdipendenza.*)[26] The question was: Is it really necessary that women's politics be founded on equality with men? Perhaps not. There were also disparities among ourselves that were not recognized, and we said to ourselves: they need to be recognized and rendered into practice. How? With the recognition of authority, where the active role is played by the one who recognizes it freely in another person; whoever feels inferior sees only power.

The theme of authority was picked up by teachers and paired with a project of "self-reform" from within the school—*autoriforma*—initiated not from above but by those who worked and studied in the school. The movement of school reform—*autoriforma*—has left to us the legacy of a precious formula, "the greatest authority with the least power" (*il massimo di autorità con il minimo di potere*). Thanks to this greatest-least formula, it is possible to detect the criterion according to which the symbolic and the real can be measured in political action: it is necessary to take the real into account but, together with that and even more so, the decision about what to do and what to hope to attain must make sense, in balancing things and signs, every time.

In Madrid, in a country that has known fascism for a much longer period than Italy, a math teacher objected to me that authority, the word itself, was repugnant to her. It was a crowded room and for brevity's sake I simply answered: "Books, mathematics books included, have authority and you teach how to perceive it."

ER In short: to recognize feminine authority is crucial for women's politics and for a symbolic independence from power. Can you provide some concrete examples of feminine authority? How does it manifest itself? How is it recognized? How is this moment of recognition of feminine authority, which is not to be confused with power, detected?

LM The power that gives up its mechanical effectiveness to the advantage of authority's symbolic effectiveness is a process that can be observed, but it has the characteristics of an invisible alchemy of the essential: one needs to live it to really know it. I have practical knowledge coming from my experience at the Milan Women's Bookstore and in the philosophical community Diotima. I have integrated my knowledge with the observation of what happens on the political scene. With our feminist practice, we have understood that alchemy is activated primarily through the recognition and attribution of authority: the source of value lies in the one who sees the qualities of another person and recognizes them openly. But it is not sufficient. It is equally important that authority circulates in its recognition as well as in the possibility of receiving it and that it does not become the prerogative of someone at the exclusion of others. I have noticed that, among women, there is a certain difficulty in accepting authority, maybe due to fear of envy or maybe fear of responsibility. Among women, there seems to be less attachment to power than among men, yet there is less reluctance in exercising some form of power than in accepting authority. Perhaps it has something to do with the mother figure in one's personal life? I have had the good fortune of growing up in a family where my mother was a woman gifted with authority. Let us not forget this traditional model of feminine authority that is the mother figure. Let's not forget above all that, although the model has come to us as incorporated by patriarchy, it is prior to patriarchy and has never stopped having value in itself.

ER When Arendt distinguishes between authority and power, she draws a distinction between power as "domination" and power as the coming together of many, men and women, in concerted action.

LM It is true, as a great political thinker, she helps us read the passages in the process of alchemical transformation brought about by authority and acknowledges the important role of many men and women.

ER Arendt says also that authority is recognized by others and one cannot give it to oneself.

LM Exactly. And when others recognize authority in you, if you do not take it up, it won't be recognized in you again. It is also important to take the right measure into account: if you go wrong on the measure with reality, it is a problem. It is not possible to build theories on all of this because the situation is different every time. We have understood that whoever has authority cannot do whatever she wants. This is not authority. Authority corresponds to the reasons why others, men and women, have put trust in you.

ER The figure of the "symbolic mother" is then the linchpin of the "symbolic revolution" and, in *Non credere di avere dei diritti* (*Sexual Difference: A Theory of Social-Symbolic Practice*), we read that the symbolic mother is necessary for the translation of the feminine into the social in order not to fall into the gender-neutral code where the feminine "surplus" dissolves. In short, the recognition of the symbolic mother allows for the circulation of feminine difference, so that it does not dissipate. Thirty years after the publication of *Non credere di avere dei diritti*, how can we measure concretely the success of this "symbolic revolution"?

LM The idea of a symbolic order that does not coincide with the social order but can inspire it is ancient. Some of us have found it again in Simone Weil and have elaborated it freely and integrated it in feminism with the idea that authority originates in the maternal figure—this too is ancient but precedes or is foreign to the Western patriarchal tradition. The two ideas—symbolic order and authority of the mother—are intertwined and many women have accepted them and translated them into political practice.

ER On this topic, you have written a book, *The Symbolic Order of the Mother* (*L'ordine simbolico della madre*), translated into several languages.

LM The *Symbolic Order of the Mother* takes the place of another book that could have had the same title, but had to be authored by Diotima, that is, by the philosophical community of which I was part and with whom I was working at the time exactly on this theme as well. I appropriated it for myself, and when the book was published, I thought: if my research companions consider me a thief, they are right. Not one said as much to me, but Diotima entered a crisis due to the weakening of the collective bond based on the recognition of my authority as a founder of the community. The impasse was resolved when one among us, Chiara Zamboni, theorized that the shared work of Diotima offered its findings freely to each and all its participants. I was not therefore a thief and I declared the authority I recognized in Chiara, through whom I was tied to the other women.

"There was like a deep sigh, an assent that came from the feeling that things were falling into place. The dual bond, assumed then, put an end to the loss of the dead collective bond and gave back to L. the old authority, it gave the authority back to her by giving it to another woman."[27] This is how the story ends as presented by Diotima.

Other groups or individual women have come to similar conclusions. The theme of the symbolic of the mother appeared promptly at the moment when the figure of the father and the remains of patriarchy—understood as symbolic order that becomes law—were ending in dissipation. Within the disorder that came out of such a dissipation, in the twentieth century, the principle of the authority of the mother began to emerge, as Marcel Gauchet clearly expounds in "La fin de la domination masculine."[28]

The end of masculine dominance is an ongoing process, and "symbolic revolution" seems its most appropriate name in Western culture. Other names and other readings are possible. That which highlights the primacy of the relationship with the mother is a rediscovery for the West, whereas for other cultures it is a confirmation.

ER In the concrete example you just gave us, as told by Giannina Longobardi, the loss of authority appears difficult and very problematic.

LM In the example that I gave, I had lost authority, but it was later recognized in me when I, in turn, recognized the authority of another woman, by saying that I was bound to her judgment. This bond with another woman who had authority over me gave authority back to everyone. It is the symbolic order of the mother embodied in a situation. This is why practice is indispensable: it creates situations in which things happen that have never happened before; that is to say, you see them, whereas before you did not see them.

ER In the sense that you are confronted with specific dynamics that need to be confronted as they present themselves?

LM Exactly.

ER Language plays an essential role in giving sense to ourselves and the world. Attention to language is therefore a central aspect of your thought. For example, you speak of "living language," "mother tongue" in your books on the women mystics, or theologians in their mother tongue as you call them, and you keep coming back to language in other writings. Can you say more about the crucial role of language within your thought and give us some concrete examples of a transformation of sense, starting with language?

LM Language is the house of being, Heidegger has said. But that power dwells in language is what critical thought has ascertained. Feminism is critical thought that has brought to light male dominance. This dominance was under everyone's eyes, but they did not see it, not even the most radical critics, and I myself wanted to be counted among them.

However, feminism does not begin as a critique. It begins with the discovery that women speak. Objects of exchange, as anthropology has theorized, "spoken for" by power, and also speaking on behalf of power, yet women speak among themselves, they speak with children and with men. What do they say? I have discovered what they say "by hanging out with the feminists" and by becoming one of them, which, in the 1970s, meant telling each other experiences and thoughts that I thought not worthy of being put into words.

I remember, still to this day, the title of a book, *Le parole per dirlo*— *The words to say it*. To say what? To say the world, to say it starting from oneself, searching for and finding, in the exchange with other women—and later other men—words that would correspond more with one's and others' experience. Truer words. In this way, one comes to discover a world other than the one she thought was real and inescapable, another world in which it is possible to be free.

To me, it is of value what the writer Elena Ferrante said in a long conversation with her Italian publishers about the art of writing in her experience. Elena Ferrante said: "Il pensiero femminista, le pratiche femministe, hanno liberato energie, hanno messo in moto la traformazione più radicale e più profonda tra quelle che hanno attraversato il secolo scorso. Sicchè non saprei riconoscere me stessa senza lotte di donne, saggistica di donne, letteratura di donne." (Feminist thought, feminist practices have liberated energies that have put into motion the most radical and most profound transformation among those that have occurred in the last century. Therefore, I would not be able to know myself without women's struggles, women's essays, women's literature.)[29]

Through language, my relationship with the workplace has changed for the better, it has become more gratifying, my writing has become freer, also with myself . . . there are many examples and they are not circumscribed. There are words that I have learned to use and by using them, they act as trust in my relationships with other women.

ER Language then is key: it acts as a bridge between experience, world, and thought.

LM I wrote an essay in which I talk about Macbeth (Shakespeare).[30] He desires to be in the place of the king, but he cannot think of the possibility of democracy. He lives in a feudal society and he finds it normal to risk his life for the king. When the desire to be king manifests itself, he cannot translate it any other way than that, that is, into elective democracy, which is what will happen in modernity. This is what practice is, it is not enough to think—Macbeth thinks, but thinks badly—that is to say, there are concrete situations that demand to be thought; practice demands that we think the unthought. As a matter of fact, feminist practice has been a search for words, putting into words our desire, which then also has to be measured with reality. We need to look for the mediation, a key term for Irigaray as well. At the Milan Women's Bookstore, at the Diotima community, we have always looked for ways to combine reflection and practice. In politics, words are fundamental, otherwise force gains the upper hand.

ER In a world that is in crisis and that is facing many challenges, globally, environmentally, politically, from immigration to the resurgence of religious and political extremism, from the breaking down of international relations to the growth in economic disparity, what is the specific role of women? How do you see the future of the thought of sexual difference and of women's politics? Do you think that women's politics could become obsolete? Virginia Woolf writes, in *A Room of One's Own*, of "woman" that one day we will say, "I saw a woman today," as if she were a thing of the past.

LM Your question asks me to consider the future in light of what is still open in the present. My game is different. I do not aim at pursuing the future but at empowering the present, myself included. Among the positive factors in the current changes is the feminine love for freedom and a growing leadership by women. I do not think I need other proofs.

ER What do you mean by saying "I do not think I need other proofs"?

LM In the present, there are reasons for my happiness and for my sorrow. There is everything I desire, but not all. Marguerite Porete tells me that "what I lack is my best," because it means the possibility of a surplus about which I have no idea, but of which I feel the lack. This is enough to make the present great, much greater than a future conceived by me and by my limited resources. I'm not sure if I have made myself clear. I will recount two events.

Starting with the 1970s, I have participated in many events, in Italy, in Europe, and also outside of Europe, although rarely, due to my limited ability to speak English. I will talk about two memorable events. The first is the International Conference on the challenges of gender studies—but we can read feminism—in the twenty-first century, in Sana'a, Yemen's capital, on September 12–14, 1999. The official languages were Arabic, French, and English.

Three of us went, Diana Sartori from Diotima, Lia Cigarini, and myself from the Milan Women's Bookstore. At the time, the capital as well as the rest of the country were at peace, apart from the ongoing rebellion of some tribes on the border with Saudi Arabia, or so we were told. We were guests of the person in charge of the cultural office of the Italian embassy and his wife and were escorted by their driver, a Yemenite who was very kind, as is the entire Yemenite population. We found ourselves together with about a hundred women, and some men, mostly from universities in Arabic countries, but from some other places too, like Sudan. The city was superbly beautiful and unaware of it. The conference was exceptionally organized and it made us feel welcome in the entire city. Above all, the conference was conducted with enthusiastic frankness and vivacity. The three of us were part of the Western minority, but on more than one occasion we found ourselves in agreement with the representatives of the Islamic-Arabic world—some of them were wearing a small veil covering their face in public—in the confrontation with the filo-Western minority. We discussed freedom and sexual difference at great length. In order to get to freedom, we need to emancipate ourselves from feminine roles, some said in contrast with those who thought that there exists a free sense of difference even in the presence of different roles. I spoke in French and my French was translated into Arabic by a Syrian interpreter, a philosophy teacher.

The second event was a trip, actually, two trips, that I took on my own to Ouagadougou, the capital of Burkina Faso, in Africa, in May–June 2004 and in December 2006, respectively. Here, for different reasons, things went "badly," and I'll try to say why or, better, what I mean by "badly," by relying on what I observed during my two stays, both of a week each. The context is the relations of the Milan Women's Bookstore with an association born in 1992, Talents de Femmes, in order to sustain artistic vocations in young women, a project that is consistent with that of the Women's Bookstore. Two of the founders, Odile Sankara and Léontine Ouédraogo, contacted the library in 2002 and their association received a prize from us. They asked us to deliver the gift personally and I went.

Of that country, they said that it was very poor but peaceful and animated by a cultural life that gave rise to a political awakening in the population, in particular among women and peasants. But this was true at the time of Thomas Sankara, the young head of state since 1983, a reformer, who was assassinated in 1987. The project Talents de Femmes was inspired by that season.

I was received warmly by the women friends of the association and others, all very courageous and admirable persons who were going against the current. But it was I who, confronted with the poor side of Africa for the first time, needed much more help rather than my being able to give any political help. Actually, I was not at all up to this task and I realized this then.

ER What are you getting at by saying this? That there are concrete situations, or specific contexts, such as the one you have encountered in Burkina Faso, where your political knowledge and experience rooted in the practice of women's relations is not what is needed?

LM No, I have told you of two events in my political biography to illustrate the before and after 2001, a year when, in my view, the world turned to a global disorder in which we still find ourselves. I have told you about them to show that I do not have any illusions, but that I continue to be engaged in women's politics, that I remain faithful to my life's choice with my abilities and my limitations.

ER We are living through the COVID-19 pandemic as we speak. How do you see its impact?

LM Humanity has been put to the test with the first wave of the pandemic and, here in Italy, we thought we had been able to manage it not too badly. But now, in Italy and all over Europe, we are in the grips of the second wave, and we have understood that the real test begins now. As a matter of fact, the problems that the pandemic poses are related to those of the endangered health of planet Earth. The time of resolving problems by moving ahead, further ahead, neglecting the negative collateral effects that force us into nonviable alternatives—such as between economy and health or between freedom and social justice—is over.

The positive response that humanity has decided to look for requires that we don't look *further* ahead but *more deeply*, finding what I call the *inner passage*. This is the passage that allows for words and things to enter a reciprocal correspondence, so that we can choose for the better and not end up in a dead alley.

The pandemic invites us to look deeper and I propose that we do so by putting to work the knowledge that we have gained thanks to the women's political movement.

The recognition of women is a growing social sentiment and relationships tend toward equality without pursuing the woman-man equality in power as the goal, but in terms of the authoritative presence of women in social life.

To me and to many other women, men not excluded, it is the right approach: not promoting the power of women on par and in competition with men, but the political participation that moves from a free sense of differences, authority included. The greatest authority with the least power.

ER I realize that these questions do not exhaust your work as a whole, nor your experience as a woman, yet your answers have given us a good sense of both and I thank you for that. Is there something you would like to add?

LM You are right, but now I need to be quiet and listen. I would add only the following: if I still had had the necessary energy, I would have written—and in fact I was getting ready to write—on subjective truth. The inspiration comes from what Carla Lonzi writes on authenticity, even though this word does not belong to my philosophical lexicon. Indeed, I would have premised my writing with a citation from Iris Murdoch, a British and Irish philosopher of the last century: "To do philosophy is to explore one's own temperament, and yet at the same time, to attempt to discover the truth."[31]

ER Thank you, Luisa.

Adriana Cavarero. The author thanks Adriana Cavarero for the photo and kind permission to include it in this volume.

Adriana Cavarero is an Italian philosopher and an Arendtian scholar. She was born in Bra, Italy, and studied at the University of Padua. Honorary professor at the University of Verona, she has held numerous visiting appointments at the University of California, Berkeley and Santa Barbara, at New York University, and Harvard. Cavarero is widely recognized for her writings on ancient philosophy, political theory, feminism, and literature. Her books include *In Spite of Plato: A Feminist Rewriting of Ancient Philosophy* (Polity 1995); *Relating Narratives: Storytelling and Selfhood* (Routledge 2000); *Stately Bodies: Literature, Philosophy and the Question of Gender* (Michigan University Press 2002); *For More than One Voice: Toward a Philosophy of Vocal Expression* (Stanford University Press 2005); *Horrorism: Naming Contemporary Violence* (Columbia University Press 2009); *Inclinations: A Critique of Rectitude* (Stanford University Press 2016); and with Angelo Scola, *Thou Shalt Not Kill: A Political and Theological Dialogue* (Fordham University Press 2015).

Three

An Imaginary of Hope
(*Un immaginario di speranza*)

In Conversation with Adriana Cavarero

Elvira Roncalli You are well known, not only in Italy, for your books in political philosophy and returning persistently to the critical question of the universal subject of Western philosophy. We will talk about that, but before we delve into specific philosophical questions, tell us what important moments or events in your life have led you to devote yourself to philosophy and affirm yourself as one of the most important Italian women philosophers of our time.

Adriana Cavarero Aside from falling in love with the figure of Socrates, who struck me when I was a student at the *liceo classico*,[1] and who awoke in me a passion for philosophy, I also have had the fortune of two biographical circumstances that have shaped my way of doing philosophy for good. The first is the method of studying philosophy that I have learned at the University of Padua: reading classical philosophical texts—Plato, Aristotle, Augustine, Thomas Aquinas, Hobbes, Kant, Hegel, Heidegger, and others—in their original language. Direct knowledge of the text, and confidence with the original language, I consider still to this day an essential aspect of my philosophical work.

The second is having lived through the 1968 student revolt when I was twenty years old and therefore experimenting with the exercise—and the pleasure—of critical thought. Today they call it the "theory of suspicion," but at the time, for me, it consisted of the possibility of dismantling, decoding, and deconstructing, if you will, the philosophical texts, starting from a point of view they had not foreseen, one that was anomalous and therefore disruptive. My perspective was that of a young woman, embodied in a sexed body and immersed in a concrete life experience, who could not identify with the universal subject of philosophy and therefore saw it as abstract, and obviously also authoritarian and domineering. I discovered early on how the pretense of universality legitimizes the exercise of domination and the practice of exclusion. In short, my first approach to philosophical texts—and to their complexity, which I diligently studied in their original language—has been a critical and political approach. Everything that I have subsequently written has to do with this premise, even if to the critical approach I have added the proactive impetus of imagination.

ER In what you just said, two experiences appear to be foundational for your philosophical work: the philosophical method learned at the University of Padua, grounded in the study of classical texts in their original language, and the experience of the '68 student revolt. How do they come together in your work?

AC At the University of Padua, I was taught to study a lot and to seriously study the primary sources above all. As an Italian thinker who has studied in Italy, I am not the child of poststructuralism or postmodernism. My approach to Aristotle has not developed by way of the critique of Derrida. My approach to Plato is different from those that I sometimes encounter at international debates. The method of reading the primary texts of men and women authors, about whom I write in my books, a truly philological method, gives me confidence and assurance because I write not on the basis of others' interpretations, but in light of my direct knowledge of the texts. Now, I may be wrong here or there, and I am part of a cultural framework that conditions me as well, but the confidence in knowing the texts about which I write is there, and it gives me a certain strength.

As for '68, there are a lot of things I could talk about. When a woman like me found herself enrolled at the university, in her first year, in the midst of a revolution that stated "the imaginary in power" and where culture was not despised but, on the contrary, culture, imagination, art, and everything were viewed as valuable and as something that needed to be rethought radically and rediscovered against tradition, well, I found myself in a happy situation. On the one hand, I studied the texts of our tradition diligently; on the other, I was pushed toward gaining a critical and even radical spirit with respect to the canon of the same tradition.

ER   In hearing you talk about this, I think of Hannah Arendt, who also knew the tradition very well, was formed in and through classical texts and, at the same time, was very critical of tradition.

AC   Exactly. Hannah Arendt, as a German, studied and learned from the Greek classical texts; at the same time, she displayed an exceptional critical spirit, always at work in all of her writings and a sign of her remarkable originality.

ER   Staying with the '68 student revolt, what do you mean when you say that it was about rethinking the tradition: Do you mean to rethink the texts, critique them, and interpret them differently, or do you mean it also in the sense of changing the university as a place of learning? And, if so, how has the university changed following the '68 student revolt?

AC   The idea was of a radical change, one that would question everything. In the same way we were putting into question the relationship between father and children, likewise we were questioning the relationship between professors and students. Students were at the center and there were many self-directed seminars. It was this idea—and I say it as Arendt would say it—of direct participation in knowledge, not only as a place of learning but also as a place of creativity.

Something of this has remained, at least in my experience in Italy. Before '68, the figure of the professor was looming and, as a student, you could only study and learn. Afterward, everything became more open; for instance, it was no longer necessary to have a classical high school diploma to be able to study the humanities at the university. It is true that by becoming more open, the students' level of preparation and of knowledge has decreased. However, the opening up of universities has allowed families of modest means to enroll their sons and daughters at the university, unlike in the United States and Great Britain, where the education is classist by definition because it is too costly. I will never tire of appreciating the affordability of Italian universities, which are in my opinion of excellent scholarly level and "competitive," as they say today. Likewise, I will never tire of appreciating, especially today as we face a big pandemic, the universal access to healthcare that our public health system guarantees.

ER   Being a woman and a philosopher in the Italian academia, which is, up to this day, for the most part, predominantly male, must not have been easy. Could you say something about this, in light of your experience and what you have been able to observe over the years? How has the university as a place of learning changed, if it has changed in this regard, in the time that you have been part of it, starting as a student at the University of Padua and then as a professor for many years at the University of Verona?

AC In 1971, when I entered the University of Padua, with a research scholarship in the Philosophy Department, I was the only woman. There were many female students, but the academic world—in philosophy and, even more so, in the sciences—admitted only males. A few women were allowed to pursue their career in the literary disciplines. On the whole, however, in the entire Italian academic panorama, women were very rare and usually relegated to the inferior position of lecturers (*ricercatrici*). After several years in a precarious position, I transferred to the University of Verona, where I met Luisa Muraro and Chiara Zamboni—they too, lecturers like me—and with them I founded the philosophical community Diotima.[2] Since then, the situation in Italian universities has somewhat improved, but not significantly. The percentage of women who are promoted to the role of full professor is still very low, despite the fact that women are the majority among those who earn a doctorate. Let me add that, at the institutional level, there are no gender studies or feminist studies programs, even though these kinds of studies are done under other labels. For instance, officially I have always taught ancient philosophy and political philosophy, but my courses were often about feminist theory.

One important aspect of the Italian university today is the presence of research centers that are recognized by the university and are fairly free in their projects' thematic choice. In Verona, for example, the "Politesse Center," which deals with politics and theories of sexuality, and is directed by Lorenzo Bernini, has been active for a few years; the same is the case for the "Hannah Arendt Center for Political Thought" directed by Olivia Guaraldo. I am involved in both. Recently, a group of students at the University of Milan was granted permission by the Philosophy Department to organize a series of lectures on queer, gender, and feminist studies. Both Lorenzo Bernini and I gave presentations that were very well attended by both students and faculty. There remains the fact that today, the total absence of gender and queer studies courses among those offered at the prestigious State University of Milan appears significant and highly disconcerting.

There is a clear paradox: in spite of the international prestige of several Italian feminist thinkers who, as it happens with me, are invited to give lectures at main foreign universities, these types of programs are institutionally absent from the Italian university system, in that these areas are considered unworthy of "authentic" philosophical thought. What follows is that—to say it somewhat bluntly—many of my Italian colleagues, even if they recognize that I have a philosophical style, consider me not a "true" philosopher but "only" a feminist thinker. Luckily, there are some exceptions, but it is very telling when there appear books celebrating the so-called Italian Thought, written by Italian authors, and I am usually granted the concession of being cited in a footnote as a feminist thinker. If I were to focus my thought on postcolonial issues, as I have done when writing about Joseph Conrad, the same thing would occur. In Italy, that which is understood as philosophy, at least at the academic level, concerns itself with the universal subject and the many adventures of its metamorphoses. As such, the framework is inevitably phallogocentric and it is disconnected from the radical thought of the English-speaking intellectual community.

ER A little earlier, you were talking about the opening and the liberalization of the university following the '68 student revolt, but now, as you speak about being a woman and a philosopher in the academic world, it does not seem that much has actually changed. It sounds as if there is still a lot to do when it comes to women in philosophy, and perhaps not just in Italy. For instance, in the United States, the number of female professors in philosophy departments continues to be very low, much lower if compared to other departments and other disciplinary fields. With regard to Italy, how do you make sense of the fact that in academia and in philosophy in particular, women are few, and what do you think can be done to change the situation?

AC To start with, no matter what people say, Italy is still a very patriarchal country, and one can see it at all levels. For instance, during the COVID-19 pandemic, which struck Italy very hard, the government created a number of different "task forces," with experts in medicine, in technology, in science, in healthcare management, in economics, in administration, and so on. At a time of great and widespread insecurity, we turned to experts to confront such a radical challenge that has fiercely struck our country. During the two and a half months of the lockdown—an experience that we had not had before—our relationship with the outside world, with the rest of the country, was through television, with authoritative individuals—the head of civil protection, the head of the scientific committee, the head of the committee for the distribution of masks, for the disbursement of funds, and so forth—who informed the public on the number of deaths, on the evolution of the pandemic, and provided general information on the situation and instructions on the precautions to take. These individuals became very visible and very familiar. They were all men. Not a woman. A total absence of women, as if there were no women epidemiologists or virologists, women scientists, women economists. Yet women who are experts in these fields are many, as we know; they teach at several universities in Italy and abroad and they excel in their fields. However, let's say that, without any malice or intentionality on the part of the government, women are invisible. In a male-dominated society, when you look for an expert, spontaneously you go and look for another male. The concept of "expert" is a male, the economist is a man. Obviously, this aroused controversy and several articles were published in the newspapers about this. I signed a petition as many other women did and the most recently formed task forces have included some women. But it is not that you clash with someone who says: "No, we do not appoint women as experts," or someone else who says: "No, men are better." This is not the case. Rather, it is a real and total amnesia, because the patriarchal imaginary sees only men; it is an amnesia that is not intentional and therefore it is very difficult to do something to change it. It is a truly arduous cultural and educational operation, which affects the pervasiveness—felt as obvious, "normal," and "natural"—of the dominant symbolic order.

Pandemic aside and speaking strictly of philosophers, in Italy, the intellectuals, the so-called thinkers, tend to be self-referential toward their patriarchal order. They do not concern themselves with feminist thought, with queer theory, with postcolonial thought, with the postcultural. They live in a world that is mostly abstract and without international interlocutors, if not with those, who, like them, partake in the most traditional sides of European philosophy. Even though I was formed in the same educational milieu, I am glad to be very different, in the sense that I have always sought dialogue with the vanguard of radical international thought—and not only of a feminist kind—since the early 1990s, when I published *Nonostante Platone* (*In Spite of Plato*).[3] I have looked for intellectual and cultural realities different from my own, I have tried to understand what they meant, to understand the difference in styles and perspectives, despite the challenge of speaking a different language in direct conversations. If one confronts oneself with those of one's own culture and educational background, one is bound to remain in the same self-referential bubble, in that region of thought; the risk then is to take abstract categories and apply them to today's reality without having a real experience of what today is and of what happens in the world.

Going back to the pandemic, in some of my recent writings, I talk about it as an event that compels us to measure ourselves with a *public ethics of care*, that it becomes an experience of care, particularly intense, truly an experience of *intensive care*, as they say in English, where there are doctors and nurses—male and female—who are fighting and dying. They are dealing with actual bodies, actual deaths, which are shocking experiences. Some philosophical reflections circulating at this time, centered on the danger of authoritarianism in the "state of exception" and on the fear that the virus may be a political tool of domination, strike me in their ability to ignore thousands of these actual bodies that suffer the disease and die in hospitals, as well as ignoring the real experience of those who, day after day, look after these bodies.

ER To return to your thought specifically, what are its most significant influences and why? I am not only thinking of philosophical texts and philosophers. I am thinking also of literary works by men and women writers that are very important to you and your work, and which you integrate into your thought.

AC Homer and Sophocles are, to me, as valuable as Plato and Aristotle. Shakespeare is as valuable as Hobbes, and so on. Literature to me is interesting because it is endowed with a much richer and freer imagination, one that is much more unscrupulous and surprising than that of philosophy, which is affected by its disciplinary canon that delimits its inventive scope. Philosophy suffers the effects of the cage of rationalization. The texts by Plato and by Hannah Arendt are, however, among the philosophical texts that I have read the most in my life and that I keep rereading. I also love Emmanuel Levinas and Michel Foucault and, among the contemporary theorists, Judith Butler and Bonnie Honig. In literature written by women authors, I have a particular passion for Virginia Woolf and Karen Blixen, but recently I have appreciated the novels by Elena Ferrante and by Annie Ernaux.

Moreover, literature is important to me, because, even though I write in philosophy, I try to avoid the argumentative-philosophical style and adopt instead a narrative style. I try to organize my books around narrative modules, even musical modules, with recurring themes, organized around a refrain that generates and intersects with stories and digressions. The ideal for me would be that the book I write takes the form of the "drama."

ER You speak about avoiding the "cage of rationalization" and trying to adopt a "narrative style" instead of an "argumentative-philosophical" style. Tell us more about these two styles, how they differ and, specifically, about the "narrative style" exemplified in your texts. In what sense does it convey your way of doing philosophy, something that in itself highlights how there are different ways of doing philosophy?

AC Let me start by giving you an example. One thing that irritates me, and against which I often clash, is that if I write an essay for a volume in English that collects different essays on a given topic, the editors usually ask me not to start in the middle of the narration, but to begin with a sort of introduction where I specify what I say in the first paragraph, in the second paragraph, and so on. Even though I am an attentive reader of contemporary texts—and, let's not forget, formed in the philological method taught at the University of Padua—I usually skip the introduction even when I read a monograph. All these introductions have been written after the book was completed, using phrases taken from each chapter, and this gives me such a negative idea of the book that I prefer to skip the introductions altogether. This is what I mean, in part, by "argumentative-philosophical style": the fact that we need to treat the readers as if they did not have a highly developed intelligence and their mind needed to be guided, warning them, as if a child, about what is said in the first chapter, the second, and so on. This type of relation with the readers according to which they need to be totally guided, as if to manipulate their intelligence through arguments, explaining the logical scheme, or else they would not understand it, this I find boring and irritating.

I prefer the "narrative style," which seeks to surprise readers, draw them into the problem, into its eventual solution, even appeal to their imagination, so that readers are not bored and can see themselves as accomplices in the process of my thought. I assume that when I cite Shakespeare or Woolf, the readers know both Shakespeare and Woolf not only as well as I do, but even better than I do. If I describe a philosophical journey through a category in Woolf, I assume that the readers, as my accomplices, will be a little surprised and might think: "I had not thought about this. Let's see how it ends." This is what I mean by "narrative style."

ER In speaking of the element of surprise, you make me think of detective stories, where the reader does not know how it will end, yet along the way finds some clues that draw her in, involve her in the investigation in order to get to the solution of the mystery.

AC It is exactly what I try to do. I take a concept, I strip it to its bones, and then it is a matter of figuring out how it unfolds. I believe it could be almost a cultural trait of certain milieus, which do not go together well with what is generally understood as a philosophy book in the English-speaking world, where the author must first announce what he or she will do so that there is no surprise, the plot is immediately revealed, and the reader does not become an accomplice because the author has already said everything he or she intends to do. In this way, the reader is treated with detachment as someone who is not very intelligent.

ER Another aspect that comes to light as I hear you talking about this is the dialogical relationship with the reader. To turn the reader into an accomplice means to make her part of the story, instead of keeping her out. You seem to want to establish an interaction with the reader.

AC Absolutely. To me a text is good insofar as it succeeds in involving the reader and, in this sense, novels are much better than philosophical texts. A lot of art goes into writing a philosophical text that is somewhat narrative. If one writes a book such as *Three Guineas*, or *War and Peace*, the reader's involvement is immediately guaranteed, whereas with philosophical texts this is much more difficult.

ER Do you think that this is also due to the fact that novels involve us at an emotional level and not only at an intellectual level, whereas in philosophy, the emotional dimension is limited if it is even present at all?

AC It is certainly due to that, so much so that the challenge of philosophy, of philosophical writing as I see it, is to make it more emotional, to create a little more pathos in the reader. We find philosophical rhetoric not only in the argument, but also in creating pathos. Then, of course, philosophy has evolved in a strange way due to its origins, starting with the difference between Plato and Aristotle. Plato wrote in a literary style, imitating the theatrical style, preeminently a narrative style that is rich in plots, whereas for Aristotle we have his lectures, a very different writing style, which is flatly argumentative. Philosophy has taken the road of Aristotle, the road of metaphysical argumentative structure, and, later, by imitation, the road of modern science.

It is true that there have been some exceptions, for instance, Nietzsche, who is clearly not Aristotelian in his writings, or Schopenhauer. Even Arendt is an emblematic case: her books on *Totalitarianism*, *The Human Condition*, and *The Life of the Mind* are definitely not argumentative but narrative texts, they have a plot. She does not say first what she is going to do; rather, she opens a category, for instance, public/private, or action, and she moves freely from there. She is doing philosophy, but she has a narrative style that involves the reader. She does not have an Aristotelian style at all. Habermas, for instance, is an example of Aristotelian style. Heidegger, on the other hand, has a cryptic-esoteric narrative style, because it is difficult to understand what he is trying to say; this is also the style of some contemporary thinkers who are inspired by him. There is a Heraclitean element in them: they say without saying, and you do not know if you have understood.

ER Speaking of Hannah Arendt, she is undoubtedly a fundamental influence on your thought. Tell us about the significance of Hannah Arendt's thought, for you. What does her thought specifically offer and where do you diverge from her, while still remaining Arendtian?

AC Arendt is an example of a political thinker who is situated and unscrupulously able to read the classical texts and interpret them through a constructive critique. Arendt is anomalous and original; her method inspires freedom and creativity. The categories of natality, plurality, and uniqueness, on which her reflection hinges, attest to this. Moreover, Arendt has the courage not only to radically rethink politics, but also to do so starting from the tragedy of her present, namely, the totalitarian catastrophe. To compel thought to measure itself up with the "facts" of the present—that I consider a great lesson. Of Arendt, I accept the method and the spirit with which she questions, politically, the fundamental philosophical threads. Additionally, I take as decisive the way in which Arendt invites us to practice a materialist humanism. She does so by articulating the ontological dimension of the category of natality and the political dimension of interaction—physical and spatial—of a plurality of embodied and unique beings.

What separates me from Arendt is her substantial indifference to sexual difference and to the theme of motherhood, which is remarkable in a woman philosopher who places natality at the center of her political thought! I also find it disturbing that she undermines the social and economic issues, which she notoriously relegates to the private sphere insofar as it is distinct from the public-political sphere. About this, I agree with the fair criticism that Judith Butler discusses in *Notes toward a Performative Theory of Assembly*.[4] Butler has become a reluctant but passionate Arendtian, perhaps even more reluctant than myself.

ER   What do you mean when you say that Arendt "invites us to practice a materialist humanism"? Could you explain what you mean by materialist humanism?

AC   In the way I use this expression, essentially, I mean to say that Arendt places the human and the human world at the center of her attention, that is to say, material relationships, even embodied relationships among humans: in this sense she is a political thinker. Nature interests her little. Now and then, she writes about art and artists, but always in a marginal way. Her main subject is *the human condition*, almost exclusively. It is materialist because she gives great importance to the physical and material experience of the political, to the interaction in a public space that is physically shared.

In the history of political philosophy, starting with Plato, models of possible states come first overall, they are designs of ideal regimes that ensure or discipline order and interests. Even when we go further into modernity, the categorization of "friend-enemy" or of "dominant-dominated" doesn't do anything except reframing models already present in the tradition. Arendt, instead, keeps trying to describe the political experience in terms of concrete participation and as sharing of a public space, even when it deals with the polis—which, as we know, is not the real polis, but the polis as she imagines it. She sees citizens who go to the square, who speak among themselves, who are there present and embodied. It is precisely this emphasis on the physical and spatial dimension of the relationship among human beings, in flesh and blood, who act in concert that induces me to speak of materialism in Arendt, an aspect that I accentuate in my interpretation.

Clearly, this has nothing to do with the concept of materialism in Marxist terms. After all, it seems to me that even feminism too has a materialist tradition tied to practices, relationships, bodies, and the claim that "the private is political." Elena Ferrante as well, at least in the way I read her, is a very materialist writer.

ER   It seems that materialism, in the way you describe it, is synonymous with concreteness of experience.

AC Yes. As a matter of fact, when in the 1990s I wrote *In Spite of Plato*, the chapter on "The Maidservant from Thrace" was all about feminist materialism.

ER The thought of sexual difference, tied to the Milan Women's Bookstore (*Libreria delle donne di Milano*) and the Diotima community, has been another important influence on your thought. What does the thought of sexual difference offer that is philosophically relevant to you and your work?

AC I have never interacted directly with the Milan Women's Bookstore, but I have been among the founders of the Diotima philosophical community at the University of Verona. The texts of Luce Irigaray are, obviously, the main point of reference for the thought of sexual difference, above all *Speculum* and *An Ethics of Sexual Difference*.[5] What is fundamental in this thought is the theoretical and practical gesture of placing oneself in an embodied and sexed subjectivity, striving to elaborate a symbolic order—a language and an imaginary—that gives an account of the real experience of such subjectivity. It is not, therefore, only about dismantling the patriarchal symbolic order—an operation that characterizes, in a variety of ways, almost the entire history of feminism—but also and above all about constructing an alternative symbolic order, a feminine matrix.

For me especially, this type of constructive and generative work translated into the exercise of decoding the feminine stereotypes sedimented in the tradition, in order to give them a different meaning. For instance, in *In Spite of Plato*, I have deconstructed the traditional figure of Penelope as a faithful and submissive wife who awaits her husband, who has been gone for decades, and instead I present her as an exemplary feminine figure who not only keeps Ithaca's male power in check with her astute strategy of doing and undoing the nuptial cloth, but also gives value to the relationship with her handmaids in a space that is separate from that of men who struggle endlessly for the throne. In other words, by exploiting several "clues" found in the Homeric text, in *stealing* them in order to recompose them differently, I have tried to describe, through the figure of Penelope, some phenomena of the feminist experience such as "separatism," but also some central categories of the thought of sexual difference such as that of the "relationship among women." The sexed subjectivity that is at the center of my texts is in fact a singular embodied individual who is constituted in and through relations. It goes without saying that I take the concepts of uniqueness, plurality, and relationality from Arendt.

ER Despite the importance of the thought of sexual difference for your philosophical work, you resigned from the philosophical community Diotima, at the University of Verona, in 1990. Would you elucidate the reasons for this decision? The thought of sexual difference continues to be one of the pillars of your philosophical elaboration, as attested by your books. A likely interpretation of this separation is that there is a divergence in the conceptualization and practice of the thought of sexual difference. Is it so?

AC My resignation from the philosophical community Diotima was due to trivial group dynamics and it essentially resulted in an expulsion. I believe that my impatience toward the organization of a group that I felt was closed and self-referential—an impatience gained thanks to the '68 student revolt—may have played a part. My equal impatience toward the psychoanalytic practice and its effects on some obscure applications to group dynamics may have contributed even more to this separation.

The difference in conceiving and practicing sexual difference was already manifest in my strong desire for openness and dialogue with the various Italian and international feminist theories. I am not for reinforcing walls but for building bridges. Whoever thinks differently from me and has a different intellectual biography puts me into question and, in doing so, helps me think further. For instance, my curiosity about Judith Butler's *Gender Trouble* was immediate and goes back to the year the book was published. I think I met Judith in 1991, at a conference in Valencia, in Spain, after the publication of both *Gender Trouble* and the Italian edition of *In Spite of Plato*. We had the opportunity to meet, talk, and get to know each other and from that moment on, our intellectual relationship and our friendship has continued to grow.

As you know, Judith Butler's intellectual biographical journey is very different from my own. She moves from a postmodern and poststructuralist approach, and engages with psychoanalytical theory, whereas I do not. At the time of our first encounter, I was part of the Diotima community, where we talked about sexual difference and feminism, but we did not talk about lesbianism. The encounter with Judith Butler, who makes of homosexuality a cardinal concept for the critique of the phallogocentric tradition, was particularly interesting. I read *Bodies That Matter* with as much interest, I made sure it was translated into Italian, and wrote the preface for it. Then, a little later, while I was a visiting professor at Warwick University, I began a dialogue with British philosopher Christine Battersby, a relationship that has grown in time and lasts to this day. I deeply appreciate her intellectual generosity.

I could refer to many other women philosophers that are important to me, but the bottom line is that by confronting myself and by dialoguing with women authors who don't focus on the thought of sexual difference, and have a different intellectual journey than my own, I do not stop questioning myself and learn.

ER An important and recurring theme in your philosophical work is the critique of the universal and abstract subject of the European philosophical tradition, a subject that presents itself as neutral but affirms "Man" as the measure of the human, thus crushing and suppressing the uniqueness of every human being in their concretely embodied specificity. Yet philosophical discourse is abstract and bypasses the particular individual in order to be able to grasp what is common to all human beings. Your critique of the way philosophy has conceived subjectivity is therefore also a critique of philosophical discourse. To what extent is it possible to change the philosophical discourse while remaining within its parameters?

AC The universal and abstract subject of the philosophical tradition is a troubling fiction or, as Arendt would say, something fake. But you are right in saying that working in philosophy means to work with its abstract language and therefore risk remaining imprisoned in the cage of its parameters. This cage, however, is enwrapped in a defense net or a cloth that can be stretched or broken. Actually, the texts themselves of these authors reveal visible stretch marks. For example, the maternal figure of *chora* in Plato's *Timaeus* is defined, by Plato himself, as unconceptualizable, something that escapes any and all systematic grasps.

Already in *Speculum* Irigaray has shown how it is possible to work symptomatically on philosophical texts and break their conceptual cages, thereby generating new figures. I believe that this type of work is no longer a problem: for decades, now, various feminist theories have elaborated a remarkable and ample imaginary that regenerates itself through a language that speaks of bodies and of concrete embodied subjectivities. A great treasure! As far as I am concerned, as you have noted already, I tap into literature a lot; with its narrative and less abstract language it is an immense resource.

ER In your book *Relating Narratives: Storytelling and Selfhood* (*Tu che mi guardi, tu che mi racconti: Filosofia della narrazione*)[6] you juxtapose a relational, embodied, and vulnerable subject to the metaphysical, abstract, and universal subject. Why is it important to dismantle the universal, self-sufficient, and autonomous subject and speak of relationality and vulnerability?

AC I could answer you by saying: for love of factual truth, for giving back the sense of things that are as they are. The universal, self-sufficient, autonomous, sovereign, and perhaps invulnerable subject does not exist, it is fake. From birth, the human being is marked not only by dependence but also by asymmetric and uneven dependences. We are born and we live in relationship with others, often articulated according to unbalanced models of dependence, and we are vulnerable insofar as we are irremediably exposed to others. The problem does not lie with the negation of this fact—which is evident even in the ordinary experience of everyone—but with the need to understand why philosophy has obstinately denied it—or rather, hidden it—in the name of a sovereign subject. At the heart of this approach there lies the model of an arrogant subject conceived for domination. The sovereign subject is a belligerent and violent subject that gives shape to a political order on the basis of the idea of its sovereignty, producing hierarchies out of its verticality.

I think that many feminist theories, by insisting on an embodied, relational, and vulnerable subjectivity, although in different ways, have given an important contribution in thinking politics anew and in terms of peace, thereby wrestling it away from the warrior paradigm that has given it substance for thousands of years. This is for me a decisive aspect, and it is precisely the aspect for which, besides feminist theories, I value the work of Arendt and Levinas. I acknowledge that in my position there is a utopian vein, but utopia reinforces the imaginary of hope that nourishes my desire to think, and I hope it will appeal to young generations' desire to think as well. In other words, it is wrong to dump on young generations only the "critique" and the work of deconstruction with which feminism has been engaged for decades. The critique plays an important part but, besides that, we need an imaginary of hope that is affirmative and generative, that is to say, postcritical.

ER You have just spoken of an imaginary of hope and you have referred to imagination and to the imaginary often in this conversation. Could you elaborate on this idea of an imaginary of hope to which you keep returning?

AC What I mean when I use the expression "imaginary of hope" has to do with the following issue: men and women authors with whom I have interacted since '68 and with whom I continue to interact with, the current with which, more or less, I identify myself, is a critical current, which has become "hypercritical," practicing the so-called "theory of suspicion." This type of thought is very good at destructuring, critiquing, and deconstructing; in short, it is very refined in its destructive ability. It is, however, much less capable of constructing something that is affirmative and positive, thereby risking to give into forms of deep skepticism and cynicism that are characteristic of a certain critical attitude of modern philosophy and its vision where, generally, the future has no place. If one focuses on the critique, and even a hypercritique, it is not evident why the future should not be a pile of rubble, just as the past.

I am more attracted to a position that has now been called "postcritical," that is, a position, as I understand it, where deconstruction is done and needs to be done—because if we live in a society where patriarchy has a strong imaginary and power, the critique needs to unveil its cultural assumptions and its devices, which may even appear natural and innocent, nonintentional—but where there is also what I call a "utopian" side, a constructive dimension. The example I gave earlier of task forces in Italy with no women being appointed because the concept of an "expert" is imagined only as male concretely illustrates the mechanism at work in a patriarchal society that needs to be unveiled. You cannot just argue why this phallogocentric tradition does not work; you also need to say how you imagine a different and better society. The utopian vein is there to give hope that things will change. Let's take for instance the concept of "equality," a rather old concept that, in political philosophy, goes back at least to the French Revolution. This category of equality, even though it is always affirmed in all formal constitutions, including the Italian one, never goes to animate the material constitution because, de facto, the world is full of inequality. Thus, one not only needs to make the effort of thinking this category of equality possible for a material constitution, for a future culture or society, but one also has to risk losing one's balance in doing so.

If you have young men and women interlocutors, students and researchers alike, you have to encourage them to think in this affirmative and positive direction. If you only encourage them to be critical, they will continue to be destroyers and deconstructors and they will never gain that look toward the future that is always utopian, because the future is not yet and, therefore, is utopian by necessity. I say this, in my own way, because I do not create states or give shape to world orders. This is not what I do. In my own way, working on categories such as that of inclination, I criticize how the category of inclination has been developed in the history of the Western world and how the same category can be thought of in a positive way, in an affirmative and proactive way, both at the ontological and at the political level. What I do is limited, because neither you nor I design or create worlds but simply write philosophical works. In my craft, I follow this direction, I push in this direction and I also do experiments in this direction.

ER Indeed. I have found, especially in teaching a course such as "philosophy and gender," but other courses as well, where we read and discuss many texts that are critical of the philosophical tradition, both male and female students appreciate the critique and the deconstruction up to a point, after which they seem to reach a level of saturation and they start to ask: "What can we do to change this?" or "What needs to happen to change this?"

AC They are right. Especially because the critique, as we are doing it, is extremely refined, and also a bit artificial, repetitive, and virtuosic. When we read a text, we are immediately able to see where it is situated, whether racist rather than misogynist or colonial. It has also become a somewhat fastidious school of thought and I understand very well why students get tired after a while.

ER Thus, the critique has its part but there needs to be a constructive and affirmative part as well and the imaginary helps us think in that direction.

AC Precisely.

ER Remaining on the question of a relational subject, in the same book *Relating Narratives*, besides presenting a critique of the metaphysical subject, you distinguish your notion of the subject from the postmodern conception of the subject. You distance yourself from contemporary authors who talk about a fragmentary and nomadic subject, one that fuses with the other, and against this tendency you affirm the embodied subject. Please, say more about this important point and why it is necessary to affirm the relationality of the self, without however dissolving it in the other.

AC I think that the subject's dissolution in the vortex of its fragments is an operation still inscribed in the history of the same subject; that is, it is an internal metamorphosis, one of its late adventures. I also think that it is an estheticizing operation that, by inscribing alterity *inside* the subject, risks ignoring the other in flesh and blood, "your neighbor," as Levinas would say. As an Arendtian thinker, I have very little interest in what happens inside the self, because I think of a totally exposed subjectivity, one that leans out and that is constitutively in relation with others. In Arendtian terms, I am interested in the relational sphere of appearance, in the sharing of a world that is a space of reciprocal appearing. The fundamental question is not "who am I?," to which the postmodern question that follows is: "Is there really an I or are there not rather its many fragments?" The fundamental question is: "Who are you?" In order to rethink both ethics and politics radically, we need to learn to place the other with whom I am in relationship in the foreground, the other who appears to me and to whom I appear, the other whom I question and by whom I am questioned. To define the concept of responsibility. I do not see any other space except this commonly shared space.

ER Could you clarify the difference between unity and uniqueness? There is still a *unity* of the subject, which you want to hold on to and which you differentiate from *uniqueness*—an Arendtian concept. In what sense does this notion of unity differ from the notion of self-sufficiency? If, as you say, the subject constitutes itself in relationship with others, where does this unity come from, or how does it come about?

AC While uniqueness is a given—every human being is different from those who live, have lived, or will live, writes Arendt—the unity of the self is not given; unity is the object of my desire and others can offer me this unity by narrating my story. There is no self-sufficiency, because, as everyone knows, autobiography is a blunder, the symptom of the desire of being a narratable self with a life story that has a unity in terms of meaning. Only the other, to whom you appear in your embodied uniqueness, can ask, "Who are you?" and only the other can give you a unified form of yourself, by narrating your story. The other is always necessary.

ER You speak of a desire for one's own story and write that this is what you add to the Arendtian position. In *Relating Narratives*, you write: "Our thesis indeed adds to the Arendtian horizon the centrality of this desire. To put it simply, everyone looks for that unity of their own identity, which, far from having a substantial reality, belongs only to desire."[7] You call this desire for one's own unity "innate"[8] and on this point, in contrast to Arendt, you claim that biography and autobiography intersect as a result of this desire.

Would you elucidate how you understand this "desire," a central point in your conception of the self? What is the origin of such a desire?

AC When I speak of desire, I know that in this age of widespread use of psychoanalytic language, I am using a very hot term. Even more so, in the book, I have spoken of desire in relation to the Oedipus's story, which gets me into trouble right away. Nevertheless, I claim the possibility of using the term "desire" without having to summon psychoanalysis.

In *Relating Narratives*, as in other texts I have written, my primary field of reference is literature, that is to say, the architecture of the classical novel where we often find, perhaps as a stylistic device, narrators who relate the story of others and in so doing provide a unitary sense to their life. Why do we read novels with pleasure? Is it maybe because we desire to detect a unity in the life stories of their protagonists? Why do women friends and lovers tell and retell each other their stories, blending biography and autobiography, as if they were stories of a narratable self that desires unity? I do not wish to fall into naturalism or universalism. I do not claim that all, by nature, desire to receive the tale of their own story in a form that aspires to attain some unity. I observe that this type of desire of the narratable self is often at work in the structure of the novel and it is easily detectable in the ordinary experience, especially in women's ordinary experience.

The fundamental point at issue, again, is that in order for this desire to materialize, it is necessary that the narrator is someone else. The narratable self is constitutively relational.

ER In presenting the narratable self you also speak of a "familiar sense of every self," a beautiful expression that is not immediately evident, especially in English. Please, explain what you mean by this expression, which in Italian is *il sapore familiare del sé*.[9] What does it add to what you have already said about the narratable subject and to your understanding of the subject?

AC To put it simply, I intend to say that, in our personal memory, without having to do an explicit exercise of introspection, we "taste" ourselves immediately as narratable selves, as an embodied uniqueness who, by living, leaves behind a story. I believe that this daily unreflective experience is familiar: and it begins to be so familiar and customary to the point that it is tasted as a taste of the uniqueness of the self. It goes back to the time when our mother, or others, used to tell us, as children, about our infancy and times of our life of which we do not have any memory. By "a familiar sense of self," I mean something that is not objectivized and nevertheless has a recognizable taste.

ER Let us move on to the inclined subjectivity, which in your book *Inclinations: A Critique of Rectitude*, you juxtapose to rectitude.[10] In the introduction, you distinguish your position from the modern individualistic conception found in Kant as well as from the postmodern position of fragmentation and write: "Instead of continuing to fragment the subject, one could try—drawing on Arendt—to incline it. Instead of breaking its vertical axis into multiple pieces, one could try bending it, giving it a different posture. This could perhaps happen by inclining the subject toward the *other*—as the relational model allows and, from a geometrical perspective, even encourages."[11] Thus, by persisting in affirming the relationality of the subject, you refer to an inclined figure, typically and traditionally a maternal figure, the Madonna with child, so as to recover both relationality and vulnerability and superimpose inclination to the erect and vertical figure of the predominant subject of philosophy. How have you come to inclination and what are the merits of a subjectivity so conceived? Why is it a more appropriate model of subjectivity for a new ethics?

AC The inspiration of this book on inclination comes from a sentence we find in Arendt's essay "Some Questions of Moral Philosophy," where she writes: "Every inclination turns outward, it leans out of the self in the direction of whatever may affect me from the outside world."[12] The inclined posture postulates therefore a bending, a loss of balance of the I toward the other. To put it differently, the other is the pole of attraction that constrains the I to exit the vertical axis, which in the moral posture of a Kantian type—as Arendt herself observes—substantiates a solipsistic ethics. Incidentally, I must confess that I am very fascinated by the efficacy of visual schemata. The superimposition of the inclined posture with the vertical one is, as a matter of fact, a schema that can be very easily visualized. The history of philosophy, from Plato to Hobbes to Kant and beyond, offers countless examples of the moral and political vertical ontological model. To the extent that the inclined posture directs itself toward the presence of the other, it has seemed appropriate to me to rethink these models in terms of a relational subjectivity. To this I would add that, in everyday language, we speak of "maternal inclination"; by this, we understand a propensity in women for motherhood, as well as—and this is precisely the strong point of my thesis—a posture of the mother who bends down toward the child. In this case, my point of reference was not Arendt but rather a famous painting by Leonardo da Vinci, which portrays *The Virgin and Child with St. Anne*.

ER You also write that the idea "is to think the turn between *verticality* and *inclination*" and that "the maternal stereotype should be reinterrogated and exploited to its fullest potential."[13] Someone could object that it is difficult, if not impossible, to reinvent a stereotype that is the result of a patriarchal society that has relegated women exclusively to their procreative function. This model, then, rather than being originary, is the product of questionable subjugating forces. How do you respond to this criticism?

AC I have always worked and continue to work on stereotypes. I think that, precisely because stereotypes present the symbolic order in a condensed form, they are, at the same time, a wall to be taken down—through critique—as well as a resource to be exploited in their unforeseen power of signification—through imagination. If we abandon the self-sacrificing stereotype of motherhood, we risk abandoning also all the immanent power of the maternal figure. After all, starting with Carol Gilligan, feminist theory has shown, in a variety of ways, how it is possible to rethink an ethics of care without reanimating the stereotype of the self-sacrificing mother. I would like to add that motherhood, understood also in terms of procreation, is a decisive hermeneutical thread for reflecting on sexual difference. I'd like to say it with this formula: "every human being is born from a woman, even though not every woman is necessarily a mother." Should I give up thinking about motherhood, not only the theme of maternal care, but also *the very uncanny of motherhood*, only because I may risk falling into the trap of the stereotype? Should I give up reflecting on the entanglement of such entrails—what Maria Zambrano calls the *entraña*—where a singular body generates another singular body, tasting at the same time the impersonal process of living matter, only because I risk remaining entangled in old stereotypes? This is asking too much of a philosopher of sexual difference!

ER Let's talk about the Arendtian category of natality, which you say is her "most original category" but one that, as you write, "Arendt herself does not define with precision."[14] You point out that Arendt's attention goes from the mother to the newborn and that the birth scene remains rather cold. You write: "Her representation of natality is, to say the least, quite abstract and cold; lacking in credibility, it is almost an homage to the old philosophical vice of sacrificing the real world's complexity to the purity of the concept."[15] Tell us more about your divergence from Arendt on the question of natality and what this means for your thought specifically.

AC I find it simply astonishing that Arendt speaks of natality without ever mentioning the figure of the mother! Birth, to me, is a scene where the other is necessary, not only in the moment of giving birth, but precisely in the relationship with the *newborn*. This newborn is not only just born and therefore representing the beginning, but it is also a very vulnerable human being, in flesh and blood, who needs others, usually the mother, in order to exist. In other words, birth is a complex scene that not only announces vulnerability and relationship; rather it is a relationship between humans that is, in this case, extremely unbalanced. Compared to that of Arendt, my vision of birth is materially more realistic.

ER Arendt seeks to eradicate the sovereign subject and sees plurality, the web of human relationship with others, at the heart of the human condition. Following Arendt, you talk about a subject that is constitutively relational, exposed, and vulnerable, thereby seeking to eradicate the autarchic and self-sufficient subject of rectitude by composing another model of subjectivity. Still, why this insistence on the subject? Does one not risk remaining trapped in the Hegelian logic of affirmation and negation or even in the logocentrism of Western philosophy, in this way?

AC The logocentrism of Western philosophy postulates that what counts is the logos to the detriment of the body. The subjectivity I speak about, instead, is a materially relational, embodied uniqueness! I cannot give up the category of subjectivity because I cannot give up the ethical and political theme of responsibility.

ER Autonomy and independence are ideals that continue to exercise their appeal on the Western way of thinking. Kant's moral philosophy, for instance, is grounded in the ability of the human being to give oneself, by oneself, the moral law thanks to one's intrinsic ability to reason. Do you think that it is possible to reconcile autonomy and vulnerability or do you think instead that a disembodied subject is in itself an artificial ideal that needs to be abandoned?

AC I think that the ontology of a relational and vulnerable subjectivity is the alternative to the ontology of a rational and autonomous subject of the Kantian type. Thus, they are unreconcilable, not complementary. The protagonist of ethics, in my view, is not the self but the other. Ethics is about the responsibility toward the other.

ER Let's talk about the ethical and political question of responsibility. You refer to Levinas and to his notion of ethical relationship as being asymmetric. Thus, you bring together the ethics of Levinas with the politics of Arendt, an operation that is far from simple. Tell us more about how you see them working together.

AC Yes, it is not easy, but I try to bring them together because both give priority to the other. Arendt says that the primordial question is not: "Who am I?" but "Who are you?" Similarly, Levinas says that I am not an "I" but a "me," in the accusative; thus, here too, the priority of the other is fundamental. This aspect intrigues me a lot, because both Arendt and Levinas are Jewish, and I am more and more convinced that there is a hidden and minor current in Jewish thought, wherein the primacy of alterity is a decisive factor. It is also true that there is a problem in bringing them together. Arendt is a strong political thinker who, when she discusses ethics, does not ever place it as foundational. On the other hand, in Levinas's texts, a thinker focused on ethics, the reflection on politics is very weak. From the ethical point of view, however, Levinas is extraordinary; he has the courage of a radical ethics and we need to recognize this.

I have sought to put Arendt's politics in dialogue with Levinas's ethics, relying on a vision of ontology that I find in both—even though Levinas would never call it ontology—namely, an ontology of an exposed and vulnerable uniqueness. In particular, in rereading Levinas I have tried to accentuate the ethical asymmetry more than he does, given that even Levinas, after all, thinks according to the idea that the prototype of the human is the adult male.

I accentuate the fact that, first, in the course of any life, in our ethical relationships—and women understand this better—we are dealing with children that are vulnerable and helpless (*inerme*), with old people who are very vulnerable and helpless (*inerme*), with the sick who are vulnerable and helpless (*inerme*), and therefore, we find ourselves in ethical situations of ongoing asymmetry and imbalance that require our "inclination" toward the other. Obviously, it happens to each of us, man and woman, on the basis of the type of relationship we are in, that we exchange the ethical posture: the unbalanced situation with my old parents is different from the unbalanced relationship with my adult son, or with my husband or with a female friend or with whoever inclines toward my vulnerability. I do not believe that there is symmetry in relationships; I do not recall having had relationships that are particularly horizontal or symmetrical. Even love relationships that are relationships between two people and therefore do not require much for there to be symmetry, nevertheless they are always relationships where one is stronger and the other is more vulnerable; and then, perhaps, over time and in different situations, they exchange their roles.

There, it seems to me, the question of responsibility is clearer, because it is not the case of giving a standard response but it is always a response in situation, *in location*, and in rather unbalanced situations, wherein reciprocity is an illusion or a fictitious ethical norm. Besides, as I'd like to emphasize, if we wish to rethink a radical ethics in terms of responsibility, the postmodern subjectivity, which consists of internal fragmentations and alterations of the subject, would not be anything but an obstacle. Instead, we need to turn the I into a me, in the accusative, as Levinas suggests. That is to say a "me" who is appealed to, summoned by the other, and a "me" who responds to this call.

ER The thread of bodily materiality runs through all of your writings. One of your books is entitled *Stately Bodies: Literature, Philosophy and the Question of Gender* (*Corpo in figure: Filosofia e politica della corporeità*),[16] and there you examine that odd phenomenon for which the body is crushed by politics, but then reinserted through metaphors and figures such as the "political body." The body you refer to is a feminine body. Specifically, you talk about this in regard to Antigone, Ophelia, but also when you discuss Plato, Aristotle, and Hobbes. We find the body again in the inclined figure of the mother and also in *In Spite of Plato*. What is the feminine body to Western philosophy? Why is it crushed, expelled, denied, and, at the same time, possessed and appropriated? It would seem that, rather than eliminating it, the desire to control it and make it one's own is at play here. Am I mistaken in this?

AC I agree with you. From the point of view of the patriarchal symbolic order, there is a desire to "dispose" of the feminine body, to "place" it in such a way as to exploit it, to discipline it and control it. In this regard, let me recall Irigaray's thesis according to which in the Western macrotext we find two salient figures of the feminine: the domesticated woman and the untamable woman, one that is irreducible. By rereading Plato and other authors, I have tried to show how their writings attest to this irreducibility, that is to say, they denounce the presence of a feminine corporality that does not let herself be trapped in the system and therefore endangers its stability. The stereotypes we talked about earlier—and that can be mostly traced back to this domesticated woman—bear the traces of an irreducible feminine corporality. Substantially, I have taken upon myself the task of tracking down these traces and collecting them in order to push these same stereotypes to a different signification. In other words, I think that the point of contact—and also of attrition—between the domesticated feminine body and that of an untamable feminine body is an immense resource for the imaginary, or to use a formula, it is a decisive point for thinking a material ontology of embodied and relational subjectivities.

ER In speaking about the feminine subject, and in distinguishing her from the universal subject, the "Man" of philosophy, you underline the fact that her uniqueness lies in being embodied, having a face, a specific name, and a story that exposes her being in this way and not otherwise. Can we take this as the formula describing subjectivity, masculine and feminine, as you understand it, where the sexual difference does not dissolve into nothing?

AC Precisely.

ER Let's consider the thought of sexual difference: one of its fundamental principles is that there are two sexes and that sexual difference, the fact of being a woman, has been denied and dissolved into a presumed and generic human being that has been depicted, however, according to the image of man. Some contemporary thinkers, Judith Butler among them, are very critical of what they call the "heterosexual matrix," the notion that there are just two sexes, male and female, and no others. How would you respond to this critique of the heterosexual matrix, in light of the thought of sexual difference?

AC This is a very complex issue. Let me just preface this by saying that as a Plato scholar, I doubt that Western philosophy is born under the sign of the heterosexual matrix. I would rather say that Platonic thought is characterized by a homosexual matrix, expressed through an imaginary in which men copulate, impregnate one another, and produce philosophical logoi. To put it differently, interestingly enough, in Plato we find a normative homosexuality, whereas heterosexuality is a marginal and instrumental function for the reproduction of the species.

Having said this, I admit that the category of sexual difference evokes the binary and heterosexual paradigm, understood as giving specific attention to the difference between the male and the female, but certainly not to be understood as a model for sexual orientations and practices! After all, as I have often repeated throughout this interview, I work with stereotypes and reflect on the social and political consequences that frame and nourish them. The patriarchal tradition is notoriously characterized by a binary economy that, while disposing of and subjugating the feminine, by domesticating it into the system, nevertheless, symptomatically, does not succeed in incorporating the untamed and irreducible feminine that exceeds (*che eccede*) the system itself. In my view, it is precisely this irreducible feminine that prevents the heterosexual matrix from becoming normative.

The overall picture is very complex and demands a theoretical approach that comes from within the tension between critique and imagination. I think that the elaboration of an embodied and relational subjectivity, one that is inclined and vulnerable, finds confirmation in a variety of experiences and in a series of narratives that can be traced back to the representation of the feminine, even though in a stereotypical way.

I also think that the theme of motherhood, one of the themes I focus on in my work, necessarily implies focusing on a female body that, far from being reduced to the self-sacrificing function in the binary economy of the system, escapes it (*eccede*). Contrary to what Plato said, men do no impregnate themselves nor do they give birth, if not by way of metaphors. But a metaphor is not a body. The Platonic metaphor clearly steals the generative capacity from the female body. It is up to us to rethink this power unscrupulously.

Let me quote, in this regard, what Elena Ferrante writes in *Frantumaglia*, a text on which I am currently working: "The literary truth of motherhood is yet to be explored," and "the task of a woman writer today is not to stop at the pleasure of the pregnant body, of birth, of bringing children, but to delve truthfully into the darkest depth."[17] More specifically, "it is also essential to describe the dark side of the pregnant body, which is omitted in order to bring out the luminous side, the Mother of God."[18]

ER Let's think of inclination in relation to what you just said. In your book, your operation is to recover and affirm inclination in contrast to the philosophical tradition that does not see it as positive at all. You connect inclination also to the religious image of Mary with child, a very well-known image in Christianity. In your last answer you mentioned a "dark side" of motherhood, but it is not very clear how inclination, motherhood, and the religious image of Mary with child are tied together. Could you clarify this?

AC Ferrante writes that we need to say and put into words the dark side of motherhood and this is precisely what she tries to do in her books. We are still dazzled by the luminosity of the image of Mary with child, a figure that is very idealized and that does not allow what Ferrante calls "il tremendo" (the uncanny), that is, the terrifying side of motherhood, or its horror, as Clarice Lispector calls it. This dark side has to do with the female body, which, when pregnant, is connected with creative matter, as the threshold between being one and being two. This is something terrifying in that it consists of a singularity inside another singularity, which is the origin of a constitutive relationship and of the relationship between mother and daughter. It is in the maternal womb that embodied singularity originates.

Ferrante wants to tell the truth about the "uncanny" of motherhood, the fragmenting of living matter, an exclusively feminine phenomenon and the origin of the relationship between mother and daughter, a rather complex relationship. The "uncanny" that she is trying to put into words is generative and regenerative, like a life cycle that goes from mother to daughter, but also from daughter to mother.

The dark side of motherhood corresponds, philosophically, to speaking and naming the origin, something that the speculative eye of philosophy, in its abstract language, cannot capture and that Ferrante, instead, in her fiction and in her narrative, is able to put into words.

ER The thought of sexual difference underlines the need for a feminine symbolic. How do you understand this "symbolic"? How does it reconcile itself with the idea of embodied matter?

AC I will respond by way of Arendt: the human animal is one who has an appetite for signification. Our bodies and our lives are marked by the meaning that we give to having a body and living with others in the world. Pure matter, *chora*, something that cannot be conceptualized or signified, is the name that Plato gives to the irreducible feminine. It is here that the challenge for a feminine symbolic opens up. The elaboration of a symbolic does not consist in an abstract operation; rather, it consists in the conceptualization and narration of practices and experiences of real bodies and subjects, for the most part of a political kind, but also capable of involving the ontological and ethical dimensions.

ER In your book *Horrorism: Naming Contemporary Violence*, you use the term "horrorism" to refer to the violence inflicted on the helpless (*inerme*), those who are not in a position to defend themselves. The word "horrorism," which you distinguish from "terrorism," is the word you coin to describe the condition of the defenseless (*inerme*), shifting the perspective from those who inflict such a violence onto those who suffer it. In doing this, you bring to light new modalities of violence that are characteristic of our time and that have their roots in the wars, massacres, and genocides of the twentieth century. Through your analysis of horrorism, you also call for a new ethics, one that is not disembodied but that is founded on the suffering of the helpless (*inerme*). Would you elaborate on what would be the principles of this ethics?

AC More than on violence, my analysis insists on the position of the defenseless (*inerme*), their being the target of a unilateral violence perpetrated at random. Today's horrorist violence strikes anyone, in the sense that it turns its victims into causal victims, giving them the ontological and dehumanizing status of "whoever." In this context, which is a specific context of extreme violence, I see the necessity of a new ethics that sees human vulnerability as its primary reference. I am not alone in feeling the need, today, of thinking of an ethics—and a politics—of the defenseless (*inerme*). My particular emphasis, perhaps, is on the defenseless (*inerme*) as an example of absolute vulnerability that is totally dependent on the care or on the wound that comes from the other. With Levinas, I keep thinking of the ethical relation, not only as an asymmetric relationship, but also as a structurally unbalanced relationship. My idea of ethics is inhabited by embodied and vulnerable singularities who are totally exposed to the other, to the violence or to the inclination of the other. There are no autonomous subjects of the Kantian type in this ethical framework!

ER In *In Spite of Plato*, you employ the "tactic of stealing," that is to say, you snatch the feminine figures from their context and in doing so you reveal the conceptual threads that have imprisoned them; you free them and make visible other significations, giving them back to a feminine symbolic, which refers to an originary maternal figure. You write that you have learned this strategy of stealing from Arendt: Where, in particular, do you see it at work in Arendt? What are its merits that you find so effective in your way of doing philosophy?

AC From Arendt, I have learned the method of exaggeration, which consists in elaborating a thesis and pushing it to its extreme consequences. Her anomalous interpretation of Marx—about which I have also written a brief essay[19]—is a good example. Also, her thesis in *On Revolution*, according to which the American Revolution, and not the French Revolution, is the real revolution. Arendt challenges the canons of traditional interpretations and, moving from a new idea, for instance, that of the relation between natality and action, reconfigures in an original way the conceptual constellation to which these interpretations had given an order. For me, working on stereotypes means to adopt the courage and the unscrupulousness that this method gives me.

To my students who would like to pursue philosophy, I say that there are two kinds of ignorance. The first is that of someone who has not studied and does not know. It can be overcome by studying the philosophical texts carefully and with adequate philological tools, by exploring the related bibliography and the critical literature on the topic. The second kind of ignorance consists in trying to forget what one has learned, that is, in the effort to think anew and freely the issue at stake, despite the immense bibliography we know on the topic. It is at this point that, if one has a good idea, the intellectual imagination becomes productive and generates philosophical narratives that are interesting and original.

ER In times when democracy is in a crisis and under attack by all types of populism, prevarications, and abuse of power, you have just published a book entitled *Democrazia sorgiva* (*Surging Democracy*),[20] in which you revisit the Arendtian concept of the political, now more actual than ever. In this book you contrast the voice of plurality with that of the masses. Why do you dwell on the "voice" and what is specific to the voice of politics?

AC This book is ideally a continuation of my book *For More than One Voice* (*A più voci*),[21] where I suggested the necessity to thematize "a politics of voices," an issue that I did not elaborate in depth there. The context of my thinking in this new book is in fact the contemporary crisis of democracy but, above all, the commendable effort by some contemporary philosophers—such as Abensour, Butler, Rancière, and others—to rediscover and "save" the fundamental core of the idea of democracy by qualifying it as "radical," "insurgent," "antagonistic," and so on. I have decided to qualify it as "surging democracy" and, by this, I mean those experiences of plural interaction in a material space that is shared—the political squares of the Occupy movement, of the Arab Spring, or, more recently in Italy, of the *sardine*[22]—that take the shape of a democracy in its generative phase, that is to say, a democracy in its nascent state that allows its participants to "taste" (*assaporare*) the emotion of public happiness. The category of "public happiness" comes obviously from Arendt, as does the category of "plurality," which is indispensable for defining the concept of surging democracy.

Rereading Judith Butler's *Notes toward a Performative Theory of Assembly*, and in seeing the squares fully packed by a collective subject, in my book I raise the decisive question of how to distinguish plurality from the mass. There is an enormous amount of political, sociological, and psychoanalytical literature on the theme of the masses, but the theme of plurality is essentially a theme of clear Arendtian matrix. I tried to distinguish plurality from the mass in light of different soundscapes that they produce, that is to say, the different soundscapes that characterize the emission of plural voices as a pluriphony (*plurifonia*) and that of the masses as a single voice. In other words, I focused on our ability to distinguish the tone of public happiness, which resonates in the participative music of plural "assemblies," from the menacing tone of violence and aggression that vibrates instead in the vitalistic music of certain vocal crowds. As you know, the issue of vocality is very dear to me because it involves the body directly, the physical and bodily emission, an element that goes well with the material, spatial, as well as bodily and relational dimension of the surging democracy. Symptomatically, in this book too, I let transpire my predilection for literature and I engage texts by Roland Barthes, Elias Canetti, Boris Pasternak, Emile Zola, and others, in different ways. Philosophy rarely deals with the theme of the voice, whereas literature is very rich on this topic.

ER I would like to reflect for a moment on the significance of political interaction and participation, on the concept of participatory democracy that you take from Arendt and that you elaborate in *Surging Democracy*, and specifically on the joy that emerges from this participation, the so-called "public happiness." How do we think about this interaction in a time when, with a pandemic, we are all locked at home? How does this affect political interaction? What form does it take? How does it change? And if it does not change, how does this joy in political participation live on? This emotion of "public happiness," now absent, how and where does it manifest itself?

AC As a matter of fact, I feel it in the form of a nostalgia. It is not the case that I have changed my idea of surging democracy. Yet as it implies the coming together of bodies, seeing each other in the face, and the joy of a plurality of people sharing a common space—precisely what is forbidden at this time—the idea of "surging democracy" may appear somewhat paradoxical. It is paradoxical not because the theme of relationship is not there; on the contrary, in times of physical distancing, it is very strong, in that each one of us is potentially an infective subject. We are in a relationship with the community precisely because we are possible vehicles of contagion. Distancing our body from others' bodies and wearing a mask are acts of care toward the other, that is to say, they call for a *public ethics of care*. Obviously, there is also the element of self-preservation, of the fear of not becoming infected by other bodies, but, at least in Italy, the general awareness is that isolation and the mask are tools that help protect especially the community from infection, protect the most vulnerable bodies, those of the elderly or those who are particularly exposed due to their social or health conditions.

Nevertheless, not everyone has understood that the pandemic imposes individual and collective participation, what I call a *public ethics of care*. Some young people, for instance, as soon as the lockdown was lifted, rushed to congregate in bars or in places of nightlife despite the fact that government ordinances, as well as a civic conscience, prohibited this. I have heard these young people interviewed on TV, especially young men I must say, who said without shame: "I'm not afraid of the virus." Whoever says, "I'm not afraid of the virus" is obviously an egoist who thinks of himself not as an infective subject, but as a subject that can be infected and therefore issues his manly challenge, "I'm not afraid." This is an exemplarily egocentric approach because it places the I at the center and ignores the existence of the other. On the contrary, even in times of pandemic, it is always the other, in this case the community, that is the point of reference, not the I.

The time of the pandemic is, however, a very paradoxical time, in which relationship means distancing. Even more paradoxical, just to answer your question, is to think, at this time, of the experience of surging democracy, which brings together bodies in a public and shared space, or even to think of love or of many other forms of relationship. In all of these instances, it is always a question of relationships of bodies in proximity and not at a distance. I truly miss this relationship of proximity. I feel a sort of nostalgia, the nostalgia of a possible public happiness. A desire that cannot be actualized at the moment because, at the moment, we are living the paradox in which relationship means distancing.

ER   It would seem that in the present context, we need to become more creative and think about other forms of interaction. Many speak about returning to normality; they yearn for life to go back as it was, get through this difficult time, and return to how things were before. Others, instead, emphasize how the pandemic has shown that what we took for "normal" is actually problematic and that our way of life needs to be thought and rethought anew, and this also goes for our being together. If the possibility of a contagious virus and a pandemic were to become more regular, something that we need to learn to expect, how does our being together, our political interaction, and even our human condition change? Do you see this as something transitory or do you see this crisis, which has forced us to take drastic measures, as something to think for the future, that it could occur in a more or less frequent way?

AC   I find the latter hypothesis somewhat pessimistic. Human history has known many infections, starting with the plague of Athens at the time of Socrates and, later on, in the Middle Ages and in modern times, there have been other periods of plague until the Spanish flu—and my grandparents lived through that. All of these are known and we have learned about them. Now there is undoubtedly an increased probability of pandemics due to globalization, but we cannot think that our standard of living is an ongoing pandemic. I am among those who hope to return to normality. It is clear that we need to understand what we mean by normality. Some aspects of normality, the negative aspects, have become more pronounced with the pandemic, for instance, aspects of inequality. Thus, in returning to the so-called normality, we should think about a normality with less inequality, a normality more attuned to the concept of surging democracy, free from racism, sexism, and all forms of domination, for example.

Then there is also this economic verb that rules in all countries, Italy included; the market quivers and presses. After the shock of the lockdown and the number of deaths, and while people kept dying, the most common phrase one heard in Italy, uttered by many opinion journalists, whatever their political tendency, left and right, was: "In order not to die by way of pandemic, we will die by way of the economy," meaning, we will starve to death. Therefore, the economy needs to get going again and so does the market, at all costs. There is this dictate of production that has resurfaced even stronger than before and has not been tarnished in the least by a pandemic that has caused thousands of deaths.

Everything is restarting as before with somewhat different problems, depending on the country and on the type of economy. Certainly, the area that has been most heavily struck in Italy, the north—some scientists say it is also linked to pollution—is the most economically advanced part of the country and it is also the part of Italy that absolutely wants to start again and return to how things were before. In fact, having lost three months of production, we need to produce even more, they say. There is this idea of capitalism as infinite production. Thus, there are no good signs that this concept of capitalism as infinite production is being rethought.

However, surely the pandemic experience would be the opportunity to rethink it, to rethink the distribution of wealth, to rethink work, how we work and its inequalities. For instance, I have heard that business and restaurant owners in Venice have complained because cruise ships do not come to Venice anymore, and therefore there aren't thousands of tourists who disembark from cruise ships and go buy plastic gondolas, or their sandwiches at the bar. The fact that large cruise ships come into Venice's canals is in itself rather shocking, given how large they are, and it is something that makes you think and hope for another "normality." Yes, we have the opportunity to think differently about what we thought normal: the type of economy, inequality, the big cruise ships, tourism. For you in the US, it might entail rethinking the healthcare system, which in Italy is good, as you know. But, unfortunately, there are no propitious signs that this kind of rethinking is happening, at least for the time being.

ER Let's return to the important aspect of the voice in your book, *Surging Democracy*, on how to distinguish the soundscape of masses from that of plurality. Following Arendt, you write of political interaction and plurality where the distinctive uniqueness among individuals is preserved instead of there being a fusion, which is what happens with the masses, a sort of amalgamation, where it is no longer possible to distinguish individuals. The phenomenon of singing from balconies that we saw everywhere in Italy, during the pandemic lockdown, how do you interpret it, more on the side of masses or on the side of plurality?

AC The singing from balconies is not a political interaction. The singing from balconies is to show each other a nostalgia for something that is lost, for the loss of relationships of proximity. It is a song of solidarity and at least, as Bonnie Honig insightfully suggested, a "serenade for democracy," for the participatory politics we did miss during the pandemic more than ever. As you know, Arendt is not interested in vocality, whereas I am very interested in the sphere of vocality as a political sphere, in political soundscapes and their emotional weight. Everyone knows—even politicians—that we are dealing with political emotions when dealing with vocality in the political sphere. Not for nothing they invented anthems; not for nothing there are war marches; not for nothing every party, every group, has its song, because the collective song allows one to feel, empirically, the experience of union. If we wanted to employ anthropology or neurology, we would say that maybe there are deep layers in our brains, and an emotional one for belonging to the group, for the collective belonging. I, at least, I feel this because choral singing moves me every time.

As a premise, what interests me is vocality as a place of strong political emotionality. I have tried to distinguish at least two types of emotions tied to the phenomenon of vocality. The emotion that is described more often is that of the mass singing in unison, where unicity dissolves and becomes an amalgamation as you say—I have chosen Canetti because he writes about this abundantly. This phenomenon is well known and Canetti describes it very well, he speaks of "how gladly one falls prey to the crowd," of how he, on several occasions, "became a part of the crowd and fully dissolved in it."[23] As a matter of fact, such a dissolving is actualized empirically in singing in unison very loudly.

It seems to me that public happiness, if observed from the perspective of vocality, belongs instead to plurality, namely to a singing where everyone keeps their singular voice, where the element of collective unity is less strong and the emotion has to do with the sonic interaction among vocal unicities. I found the anecdote Arendt tells us about Pasternak, of which I talk in the book, to be a good example of what I mean by "pluriphony." As Pasternak reads one of his poems in a public room in Moscow, he stops because his sheet of paper falls to the ground and the people who are there, spontaneously, one by one, and then all together, continue to recite the poem as if in a choir. There is something really intriguing in this anecdote, because there is community, there is resistance, there is uniqueness of voices that come together and become a choir; but it is not a mass, they remain a plurality. It is, however, the emotional element that interests me in the vocal phenomenon. It can be the singing or other rituals, some of them really fearsome, as we know. In being just one vocal body, in singing in unison, there is obviously a very dangerous emotionality, readily available to the first dictator that appears on the scene.

ER When you speak of "public happiness," of the joyful emotion that one feels by being part of a plurality that does not erase unicity and distinction, it seems that in describing it, you exemplify the condition of being free from needs. In other words, a condition where one is not concerned with necessity, something for which Arendt has been criticized a lot. Butler, among others, does so in her *Notes toward a Performative Theory of Assembly*. Tell us more about how you understand "public happiness," and where you stand on the question of political participation with regard to needs and necessity.

AC Arendt also says—unfortunately—that the ancient Greeks were able to discover the authentic political experience, because they had slaves and, therefore, they did not have to concern themselves with needs. Translated into our time, and for us, who, fortunately do not have slaves, we can rephrase the Arendtian thesis about the centrality of political action by noting that there are moments of the day or of the week when we work and do what is necessitated by needs; women know this even better than men. But at the moment when we go to the town square and interact with others in a public space, that is, at the moment we participate in the experience of surging democracy, well, in that moment, our body is not the body with needs but the body with political emotion, with public happiness. I don't think Butler has considered this. There are political experiences in which the body is not the body with needs. Certainly, the body is there in the square because either the one who embodies it, or someone else, has provided for its needs. Yet in the specific moment of going to the square, in the moment they expose themselves, interacting with other bodies in a public space of appearance, they do not present themselves as a body with needs.

ER One of the repercussions of this pandemic is that the burden of care and sustenance of our bodies has fallen, to a greater proportion, more on women than men. Women have been more heavily and negatively impacted by this.

AC In Italy too, we have had a lot of discussions because by closing down schools, it is above all women who have taken on the burden of care, domestic work, and so on. In Germany, some women have come together and have demanded a salary from the German government, because, as they argue, during the lockdown they are contributing to the German economy, at home, as the ones who look after bodies, children, and so forth. Even though, most likely they will not be successful in this, their action is valuable from a symbolic point of view. This is highly debated in Italy as well and it is a very complex issue.

ER The critique to Arendt and to her notion of politics, that is, that politics is not about needs, gives rise to much criticism, and rightly so. It has to be thought seriously, just as the private-public division, or what politics is about, as you do, for instance, with the concept of "natality." It is also the case that when you look at it from the perspective of those on whom the care of needs has been imposed—above all, women, who have been charged with the care and sustenance of bodies as if it were their "natural" destiny—the liberation from these needs looks like the fundamental point, rather than our needs being what politics is all about. In other words, although the care of our needs is essential to the human condition and cannot be denied, it is not what we are busy with when we are doing politics. And this raises the obvious question of who looks after our bodies? How do we manage the care of our bodies?

AC It is necessary that we all take care of them, men and women, and in moments that are not political. But Arendt is not clear on this. As I have already said, however, I do not share Butler's position completely either. First of all, the fact of appearing in the public space as a body with needs is not consistent with my personal experience. My experience of public happiness with the *sardine*, with the feminist marches, or with all the places where we have shared public happiness, have not been experiences where at the center was not a body with needs, but instead the emotion of a body liberated from needs. One thing is the gay claim, the gay pride, a minority that shows its sexual orientation, that demands equal rights, that does not want to be excluded, and wants to fight in the name of their gender identity, which they perform in and through their bodies. This is part of fair political demands. Politics is this too; but the political experience tied to the pleasure of interaction with a plurality of unique beings, who are unique and equal, and which I call "surging democracy," is not just this. What Butler does is very interesting, but the body with needs that is central to her thought is also what works a bit as an anchor, in the sense that it prevents her from seeing the joy of public happiness, the political emotion of acting in concert, independently from needs.

ER What are you working on at the moment?

AC I'm still working on the theme of democracy and vocality because, following the publication of my book in Italy, some journals have asked me to write essays on this topic. Additionally, I am writing a paper on the uncanny of motherhood, where I grapple with texts by Elena Ferrante and Clarice Lispector, to be presented at an international conference of the Society for Italian Philosophy (SIP).

ER As a critic of Western philosophy, yet a philosopher yourself, how do you see the future of Western philosophy? And the thought of sexual difference?

AC I am an optimist because I have much faith in young generations. In my meetings with them, I find in the young the desire to produce an innovative philosophical thought, one that is attentive to the bodily dimension and to the concrete experiences that they are living, in an ethical, political, and an environmental sense. I believe that a materialist and pacifist humanism, open to the serious and looming ecological issues that grip the planet today, can help the work of philosophy to overcome the fences of its, by now, tiresome jargon.

ER Who is Adriana Cavarero when she is not doing or writing philosophy? What are your other passions besides philosophy?

AC I love to sing, to dance, and I am passionate about music. With age, my emotional side has grown. Now, I get emotional to the point of tears when I listen to music and when I gaze at works of art in museums. I go to concerts and museums with a handkerchief in my hands, faking a cold, because I am a bit embarrassed by my exaggerated emotionality. I read a lot of narrative, about three hours every evening before going to sleep. I love to walk, but I hate physical exercise and playing sports. I was born in the countryside, but I feel at ease only in big cities, especially New York, where I enjoy the plurality of cultures, ethnicities, and languages, even in a simple trip on the subway. When I visit a place where I have never been or where I have been only a few times, I never have a preplanned program and I do not shut myself up in museums. I walk around, stop for an aperitive, talk to the butcher; that is to say, I want to see and smell the smells of Madrid or of whatever city I happen to be in. If then one day it were to rain, I may also go to a museum. I am not very sensitive to natural landscapes. As my late friend Hayden White used to say, "In nature there is no plot."

ER This makes me think again about what you said earlier about the narrative style, that it needs clues in order to involve the reader.

AC Yes, "there is no plot in nature." It is culture that is filled with plots, even though we tend to unload plots on nature. Even the COVID-19 virus now appears like a "plot" to us.

ER A life that is clearly "distinctive and unique," as Arendt would say. Of all that you have been able to accomplish and that you continue to accomplish, is there something about which you are particularly proud? Would you change anything, if you could?

AC Every human being has his or her unique and distinctive life. Uniqueness is not exceptionality. I do not feel exceptional at all. More than proud for what I have been able to do, I am grateful for the fortunate opportunities that life has given me. I have met wonderful and intellectually generous people who have appreciated what I do and have helped me. I would not change anything even though I obstinately continue to hope that, sooner or later, we'll find an efficacious way to change the world in the pacifist sense.

ER At the conference in Brighton in 2017, held in recognition of your philosophical work "Giving Life to Politics: The Work of Adriana Cavarero," following an open debate with Judith Butler and Bonnie Honig, you said this more or less this: "I want to work with feminist women who are building an imaginary of hope and peace, who promote relationships grounded in altruism and in an ethics of care. We need to be optimistic in order to build a society founded on peace and nonviolence." These words can be taken both as a reflection on your philosophical work and as the central principle animating your thinking. What do they mean for you specifically?

AC The elaboration of a feminine symbolic order has always meant, for me, the commitment to promote an imaginary of peace and hope, against violence, wars, injustice, suffering, inequality and now, ever more pressing, the life of the planet. I know that this may sound utopian and, maybe, even banal. But we need not fear the banality of pacifism and of the desire for a better world! What today is understood as "realism" generally corresponds to a disenchanted "cynicism" according to which things are as they are and cannot be changed: in the global world, the wealthy and the powerful dominate, violence and oppression dominate, the poor and the outcasts suffer, the migrants who flee from unlivable situations increase, the market and economic interests rule—and so it is. "Realism" would consist in explaining and justifying the existing reality, without wasting any time in banal and therefore ridiculous utopian instances.

On the contrary, I think that the history of feminism itself and of other radical movements attest to the fact that oppressing mechanisms can be changed, that the world can be inhabited by diverse, positive, affirmative, and nonviolent subjectivities that are characterized by the will to live in peace in the name of plurality. It is here that the imaginary plays a crucial role. Let me say it with a rather drastic expression: only by imagining the impossible, can we make it possible. This is the formula that has always accompanied my philosophical work.

ER I am aware that there is much more to talk about, when considering your entire work, that we have not talked about in this conversation. Having said this, is there something in particular or an issue that you think important to discuss?

AC No, I have spoken even too much and your questions have touched on all the main themes of my thought. Thank you.

ER Thank you, Adriana. It is always a pleasure to converse with you.

Rossanda Rossana. Photo by Carlo Leidi. The author thanks *Il Manifesto* for the photo and kind permission to include it in this volume.

Rossana Rossanda was born in 1924 in Pola, now Croatia. She studied philosophy at the University of Milan with Antonio Banfi and graduated in 1946. She joined the antifascist Resistance in 1943, and in 1959 was called to be part of the Italian Communist Party's Central Committee. She was responsible for the cultural office of the Communist Party in the 1960s. In 1969 she was expelled from the party together with others of *Il Manifesto*, a newspaper of which she was a cofounder. A journalist and a writer, she is the author of many books, among them: *L'anno degli studenti* (De Donato 1968); *Le Altre: Conversazioni sulle parole della politica* (Feltrinelli 1979); *Un viaggio inutile* (Bompiani 1981); *La ragazza del secolo scorso* (Einaudi 2005); *Questo corpo che mi abita* (Bollati Boringhieri 2018). She died the 20th of September, 2020.

Four

Selected Essays by Rossana Rossanda

The Unrepentant Emancipated Woman[1]

In front of me is the reproduction of a portrait from the 1920s: it is Anna Akhmatova, painted by Nathan Lothman.[2] I had never seen it before. Anna is sitting on a couch, where she rests her long back, and her wide neckline, with her very long legs crossed, and her severe profile slightly leaning forward with the hint of a smile. For the rest, she is collected, a little reserved; one who has chosen herself, from the straight posture of the head to the little low-cut shoes. Like a Chanel perfume that spreads beyond all ideological borders, the feminine body has become free and thin. A new body, like the times.

She is an emancipated woman. Why does she appear seductive to me? Because of some sort of a happy and also curious confidence that goes through her; she is breathing what Moscow believed to be, in the circle of intellectuals that mingled with an astonished crowd full of hopes, a revolutionary turning point. The river of history runs within the person; she, a woman, a poet, was a segment of that uproar of novelty, of discoveries of ideas and forms, of liberation of the person and of the word—Lothman, the one who paints her, is a friend of Lissitzky. This long and reserved figure, is she a perfect male? Good god, we can say everything except this. But she is not a female representative of the dominated and hurting sex either. Her sorrows, which later were many and did not bend her, acknowledged only the inner tribunal of their forms, I believe.

Many years later I would meet her, with her body disjointed by age but with that ironic folding of her lips still unchanged. She closed them harshly for me, with a flicker of annoyance, when I was introduced to her, at an embassy, as "the one in charge" of communist intellectuals. That was enough, I knew her kind and I did not try to explain to her that I was "different."

Today, that 1921 image of her hangs on the wall behind the computer on which I am writing about emancipation and, with that smile, it challenges me to say that she was a simple, foolish, and subordinate female subject. Yet the feminist critique of emancipation persuaded me and persuades me still.

It persuades me as the critique of something that is "not enough." But I will not repudiate Anna and write that her force was illusory. It was a force, and unless one goes through it, every "surplus" of liberation is illusory as well.

So I think. Is it my personal story that obscures my thinking? I am twenty years younger than Akhmatova, perhaps more; but women like me have still known a moment or two of that joyful stretching of oneself over everything, having shaken off one's back a sense of oppression, and feeling free and responsible. And also, yes, feeling alone, because solitude has its pride and advantages. There was something a little bit Luciferian in being a free woman, and one among a few women. The challenge with men became also a challenge with the past from where we came and where other women remained. Did we have so little solidarity with those women who stayed in the past due not to a Luciferian but rather a Satanic conspiracy with man against all other women? The humiliation of the other women faded on us. We were more inclined to the fury "against" than to an understanding "for." I believe that this accent can be found in all emancipated women until they first encounter a feminist demonstration.

From this, we would go on to the discovery of feminism or of feminists, not without difference, and, later, enthusiasm. We would learn something from them, and we would have liked to tell them something else. We learned that there was an area within ourselves where the freedom we thought we had acquired was not entirely such: the terrain of an ancient dependence on sentiments. Not that we had not perceived that which, by then, seemed to have become an inscription in the feminine being; however, by negating it, we felt more transgressive than authentic. Therefore, we were led to realize ourselves more as "persons" than as "women"; woman had in fact been so shaped by what women had been or what perhaps they were (we were), and which we did not like, that we preferred to put ourselves aside with respect to some profound levels and pay for this renunciation.

We had learned not to love ourselves and from the feminist movement we learned that ourselves, and that this was, actually, perhaps the greatest transgression.

Under the condition, it seemed to us, it seems to me still, that we would revalorize ourselves by continuing to cut short every concrete dependence. In this, we wanted to be "like men," self-sufficient, and we found ourselves in the struggles or in the protests of those who felt banned, coerced into not being self-sufficient. And then we spurned what still seemed to us a dependence, this time a dependence on our own historical image, which seemed to us to manifest itself tenaciously in many new feminists. It consisted in changing the sign, from "minus" (negative) to "plus" (positive), to what women had always been, that is their being confined to a horizon made more of sentiments than of intellectual adventure, within the *hortus conclusus* of only interpersonal relationships that became the place for perfect narcissism, for self-reflection in seduction, for low power. There was a sort of pampering ourselves—in round dances, in fluttering skirts, in the odds and ends, in the "woman is beautiful" slogan, in the exuberance of the color pink—which seemed discouraging: a short and ambiguous provocation.

To cut short meant to meddle in the world of men, to know their rules and to fight in order to change them. It was simpler to believe in this approach for someone, a communist, who would meddle and uncover her cards. We wanted to change, and we saw in the sexual division of social labor a form, if not "the form," of feminine dependence, which extended beyond the centuries and founded the sphere of the unwritten (or, not always but at times, also written) domination of patriarchy. With this approach, we thought that we could escape male conditioning. Above all though, wide fields of urgencies, commitments, and obstacle courses were opened up.

This interested us. It interested an emancipated woman, which was not necessarily the same as a "go-getter." Above all, two things were pressing: how to escape the conditioning of the ancient division between site of history and site of the family, a place of doing, and a place of being, site of a wide range relationships and site of in-depth relationships. These could be liberated in terms of their possible values, we thought, only on the condition of escaping the coercion to repeat the obligations of social reproduction (the necessity of providing nourishment, enabling rest, care-taking, inhabiting a house, everything out of duty, "natural" duty, rather than out of free choice). Objectively, this rendered the sexes dissimilar in power, in knowledge, and in the order of decisions, burdening women with a double obstacle in terms of their ability to matter. Namely, formally, for thousands of years but also up to this day (even though no longer formally), women have been, first, excluded or challenged when trying to enter the sphere where decisions or stipulations regarding the living conditions of citizens are made and, second, they have been subjected to an unwritten law in terms of family relations.

The second matter of interest to us was how to read ourselves, as an uncodified presence, in history, in its images and symbols. We had, in fact, been strongly "thought about," not at all reduced to the "neutral" of a universal sex with an appendix, but thought about in a specific, and even ambitious, role of emotional compensation, a maternal womb even when sterile, a place where man finds himself and receives self-confirmation. We had no doubt that this was a "power" that had been given to us; perhaps even thanks to this power, we had accepted a partial idea of ourselves as "individuals," yet no idea at all of ourselves as "women citizens." Powerful and irrevocable as mothers though, as the secret and passion of the "feminine," a place where he could even lose himself.

To the emancipated woman, this asymmetry within the couple seemed an obscure node. For this reason, perhaps—much more than out of admiration for the other sex, which we knew well at work and in politics, that is, in his hunting grounds, and which thus impressed us little, as we had rapidly learned to hunt like him, sometimes better than him—it was hardly the case that a true emancipated woman would be in a harsh struggle with a man. Whereas it was not impossible to defeat him on the terrain of history (we only needed time to invade it with many women), we did not want to defeat him with the classical weapons of the maternal command, of seduction, of our "different" body, which, in modern times, everything was teaching us to consider more beautiful, sweeter, more full of charm. The emancipated woman dressed severely, she did not want to exhibit herself; maybe, within herself, she chased an idea of an equal relationship, two who recognize each other—some of our female friends would say, two androgynous individuals.

What remains, in the emancipated woman's self-awareness, after the new feminism? I believe that what remains is an ambiguity that is not fruitless.

She is tied to the "lived experience" (*vissuto*) of feminism, by the discovery, in the narrow sense, of sexual contradiction as something that can be broadly articulated within the social division of labor, but is "not" reducible to it. Nor is it completely reducible to history, because such a long and homogeneous history empties itself out of what characterizes history, that is, the visibility, and some rationalization of change. Not here. This contradiction has no end; the further back we go, the more we find it. Actually, socially, it is perhaps more acute now, whereas in the physiology of bodies, it seemed more marked earlier. There is no mistake about the sex of the little statues that surface from prehistory. And (putting aside the exceptionality of matriarchy, about which we know little, and still, it raises the question: why is it so rare and short?) where can we situate the indelibility and the burden of sexual difference, that powerful identification that comes from within the human species, of two different genders? Why is this perceived as fundamental and constitutive, at least from the moment the species reflects on itself and leaves behind documents?

Without any doubt, there is maternity, the fact that the woman's body is the only one that doubles in another being. An experience that, at its first perception probably preceding the perception that the doubling of the feminine body followed the coupling, must have been truly traumatic for "him" even more than for "her" (for him it was an atrocious lack of a possibility, being finite). Nothing, as a matter of fact, would make visible the relation between intercourse and pregnancy, as it is not visible for children, who nevertheless know all too well that only mom gets the belly. And it is certainly from maternity that derives man's "property" over the women's body, as the only possible property over filiation, and therefore assimilable to other "goods" and more bitterly protected than other goods. And it is from maternity that comes the protection/limitation of the feminine role that we find in almost all civilizations.

A protection/limitation that is, however, entirely "human." In many mythologies, creation is presided by two sexual forces that are on a par in terms of power, one that is a he and one that is a she, and they are not uneven such as Isis and Osiris or, inversely, Ishtar and her lovers. The reduction of the demiurge to the one and male (even when the gods are many, the first god not *inter pares* is one and male) is specific to Western civilization, first Greek, then Judeo-Christian.

It is as if the "difference" as "subordination" had come at a later moment, in subsequent civilizations, breaking a binary originary schema. In the Jewish legend of Lilith, which is outside the Bible but remains inscribed in the tradition—it is still said, among the young Jewish mothers, that when the child smiles while sleeping, it "smiles at Lilith," and she is often prayed to so that she does not take it away. The first big controversy arises between Adam and the woman (a passage of Genesis allows us to think of her as created before Eve, equal and contemporary to Adam, whereas Eve will be born from one of his ribs) on "who is superior to the other." The interpreters of the tradition seem certain that what is at stake is superiority or inferiority in terms of initiative, if not in terms of the same sexual positioning. Lilith detects the nonequality of this and, rather than suffer it, prefers to abandon the garden of Eden and go "to the East of Eden," alone, cursed to give birth to children that will die, by a God that is unquestionably male and irascible.

Ever since the antiquity of the legend, it is possible to deduce that the nonequality of the sexual initiative is perceived by Jewish thought as an injustice, thus imposed through a conflict, and which a feminine sexed being in the full sense (the first of the women!) *is right* in not internalizing it.

The subsequent story will internalize it and will make us internalize it in the use, abuse, and devaluation of the woman's body throughout the centuries and until very few decades ago, when not even until now, even though in slightly more subtle forms, except for the explicit sadism of some pornography. It would not be without interest to examine how the male has lived this negation of the mother, which is present in all kinds of jokes or popular rhymes about the greater value of a cow than a wife; and even the devaluation of her sexuality, which is powerful but reduced by the pettiness of the other body.

All of this has a very long history but, I repeat, it is not reducible to history. Thus, the emancipated woman—to return to our line of thought—could not but sense an opaque point, an unreasoned threshold, something that could not be explained by custom, in the acute and irreconcilable, substantially neurotic, nature of sexual intercourse. When she in fact reads this, earlier than common sense (but the emancipated woman constitutes herself, beyond common sense as "free" sexuality, and feminine initiative) there remains, actually, there arises the thought of the unconscious, the archetype that most rigidly bears in itself difference as inferiority. Therein sex remains a burning area of the couple experience, which one tries to elude in the homosexual or lesbian relationships, even though I do not know with how much success—as if every duality were a coercion to repeat the forms of dependence, even within the same sex.

Thus, the literature is endless, not to mention the movies, about the emancipated woman who, at some point, has "to choose" between love and work; and, hard to admit, this is singularly lacking in the writings of working-class women. Perhaps, the most acute, even though fiercest, witness of this "irreducibility" of feminine sexuality is Tolstoy, though I do not know how consciously. Flaubert will place in Emma too many motivations for this irreducibility to shrink to its extreme kernel, to a story of terrible destitution of feminine love like the one that shines through, for example, in Anna Karenina. Besides, differently from Emma, Anna Karenina has what she wants and, within the couple, she snatches the rare fact that it is he who sacrifices "his" career. Nevertheless, something escapes her, something restless, unfulfilled, obsessive—and Tolstoy makes her die precisely for this. Wedekind too will have Lulu—nothing less than the spirit of the earth—killed and lo and behold by Jack the Ripper. But let us make it short. The emancipated woman knows that here, in the relationship with the other sex, at most there is a self-forgetting, an oblivion—that which is called "sexual understanding"—that is not frequent and rarely similar to other understandings.

Feminism accounts for this, to the emancipated woman, like no analyst has ever done. It is by pure polemical force that the emancipated woman is defined by the feminist woman as the pure state (you are like a man); the more she looks like a man socially, the more the emancipated woman knows that she is not a man; the differences have fallen down at work, in assets, in knowledge, in "not" being him.

And not only does feminism legitimize this difference as "thought," reason for separation, autonomy, and even a struggle, but it also projects it as a force that no emancipatory theory or science of society has had, in cultures, in social forms, in knowledge. What happened to women in the 1970s is what had happened at the beginning of the working-class consciousness, that is, a real distancing, the (split) from the other, man or master (*padrone*), placing oneself as an absolute alterity, the principle of (another) knowledge and ethics. Feminists encounter all the problems that Lukács ties and unties in *History and Class Consciousness* (how can a class that is not seen and is not thought think itself and the world to the point of changing it?) and the emancipated woman of the Marxist type is surprised that Hélène Cixous or Luce Irigaray do not quote him, nor, probably, know him. Because the difficulty of coming to be, due to having been thought by others, is a theoretical knot that begins before feminism and that women rediscover. The same can be said of the (non-neutrality) of knowledge and of language. The feminists will interpret in terms of the masculinity of knowledge and expression what the Marxist left, antiprogressive, had interpreted as (manipulation of) knowledge and expression by the dominant class. An emancipated woman that encounters feminism recognizes the two doublings.

Probably the emancipated woman's ambiguity does not lie so much in the difficulty of placing them in a series rather than in parallel: once the two contradictions are seen, the series takes shape by itself in light of common sense: that of sex comes first. But one thing is the historical location, another is the lived experience (*il vissuto*). The emancipated woman will hardly live this sexual contradiction as first, and never, I think, will she completely accept the erasure, in the "masculine," of the entire so-called "neutrality." It is like a Western Marxist in front of the Chinese cultural revolution: it is not the case that culture does not exist, either in a direct or in an indirect way, often reciprocal, just because it belonged to the dominant class; nor is it the case that, in the servant/master dyad, it does not "also" reflect the presence of the dominated and can escape it. The advent, the thought, the construct of sexual and power asymmetry is the pathway in which we move. It is immense; compared to it, any invitation to a tabula rasa, to having to rethink everything, to diffidence not as a research method but as a negation, any abstraction, of an a priori and innocent feminine absoluteness, are poor in a disconcerting way.

The will to know: Is it masculine, feminine, or neutral? The passion of the intellectual? The sense of one's own finitude? The very sense of sexuality? Living? Dying? Infinitely refracted in the differences of people, what and how far do they homogenize in "gender"? How many *neutrals* does the emancipated woman find on the road, neutrals that discolor now in the masculine, now in the feminine, dislodging planes, distances, and proportions of a scene that only now becomes, with the consciousness of the *difference* of the sexes, tridimensional. The emancipated woman remains with "identity" in the middle of the ford. In her head, she thinks that the two genders are now finally two perspectives (*ottiche*), two lived experiences (*vissuti*), two sensibilities, two levels of experience that do not ever coincide, that are never separable without mutilation.

The emancipated woman's last sin is not, therefore, that which can be overcome, of the recognition of other women: the emancipated woman is quick to find, in the woman dimension, a different communication, more captivating, sometimes harsher, in short, her own, apart. She is quick to be in solidarity. Passionate about the qualities and misfortunes of one's own sex. Among emancipated/feminist women there is talk and enjoyment, as if one had an additional lamp in a dark world. One suffers, but one does not complain. The meowing of some sisters is bothersome, or one indulges in it with contempt. The emancipated woman dies hard; hard to die in her is the problematized and thus precious neutral—the terrain that the two differences traverse, on which they transit, leaving different footprints on a beach on which what breathes is the entire fleeting sea of existence, and not only the powerful and univocal stream of gender.

A Worthy Challenge, an Assured Conflict: Women and the Polis[3]

This year has been a turning point in terms of women's elaboration: they have posed for themselves and, by reflection, for all, the question avoided up to now, namely the question of the "political." They have unfolded this word and other related ones—social, power, hierarchy, autonomy—in the many potentialities that are enclosed in the term and are not reducible to customary use. And we should not be surprised by this. From 1968 onward, this expanding and thickening of terms is indicative of the expansion of new subjects. Nor are women "one" of the many subjects that are formed essentially through the becoming self-conscious of various interest groups (nationality, placement at work, or age, etc.). They are a "gender," neither transitory nor reducible to demands for self-promotion. They are, perhaps, "the" epochal subject, in the sense of their quite recent radical speaking and for what this may imply for the future.

This attending to the political goes, in some way, against the trend of the generalized disaffection for politics. The Chernobyl catastrophe, an outcome of state powers and productive forces, has coagulated something that had already matured, and that perhaps had in common only the very question of "(political) representation" (*rappresentanza*),[4] widened in its meaning. Women, in fact, ask themselves who and what of themselves must be represented, and how.

In becoming a subject, any social figure, gives an "(ideal) representation" (*rappresentazione*) and carries with itself a change in the rules of the game of "(political) representation" (*rappresentanza*). The entry into "(political) representation" (*rappresentanza*) in turn affects the "(ideal) representation" (*rappresentazione*) that one has had up to that point. Becoming "visible" entails a difference with respect to what one was, one wanted, and one could be while invisible.

In the case of women, it is above all "(ideal) representation" (*rappresentazione*) that problematizes "(political) representation" (*rappresentanza*). In its ways, (ideal) representation is in fact received from a long tradition founded on a formally non-sexed "person." Women find themselves immediately confronted with the question: How do we represent ourselves in our specificity? Are the electoral institutions capable of highlighting "sexual difference"? Or has their historically male nature—the "polis" was manifestly a male affair, in the same way as the house, apparently, was female—not masculinized, from their very origins, the forms of (political) representation (*rappresentanza*), of the institutions, and of the state? Is it not necessary to rethink them all, from the start, rather than entering them?

This question raised by feminist groups has not disappeared for good reason. "(Political) representation" (*rappresentanza*) is a thousand-year-old problem of Western civilization, because it implies a transfer, agreed upon and revocable, of part of the powers of the individual to the associated society when the latter stops being theocratic or autocratic; that is, when it stops deriving the law from a revelation handled by a priest or a king. In the autocratic society, there is no political representation (*rappresentanza*) but "doctrine" and obedience; at most, there remain in place some precautions so that the authority, bearer of the good and the true, may not betray itself and become abusive. But when the rules of human cohabitation (and of conflict) are problematized and founded on the will of the "polis," every citizen becomes the bearer of a bill of power that will be mediated into a law. For as much as possible, that is. There is a limit, and that is the irreducibility of the person to a citizen, and of the singular citizen to a legislating assembly.

Now, the question of "who is a citizen?" has tormented political history, given that the right to citizenship is generally connected to property (or to knowledge, which generally used to go together), on the basis of the argument that the one who knows less is less able to understand one's own good and the good of all persons. Even at the time of the English revolution, the most extremist group, the Levelers, did not consider the *servant* [in English in the text] (essentially, one who has only one's arms as property) as capable of "representing" or electing a representative. And until the end of the nineteenth century and, in 1987, still not yet in all countries, it has been women who, on the basis of principles, have been dispossessed of sufficient reasoning ability to decide for themselves and for public matters.

Unlike the authority to which they were subjected in the patriarchal family, an authority that was for the most part unwritten (but also legislated by men in the key points of filiation, adultery, and property), the exclusion of women from the "polis" was explicit. If a woman was wrongly called the queen of the family, not even formally was she called a "citizen." The French Revolution, which is born with the idea of woman citizenship, dismisses it early, in spite of the irreducible women fighters and the passionate women orators that animate it, and for reason of their sex. This is known.

Less clear among us, women, is whether the indisputable maleness of institutions affects the theoretical fundament of "(political) representation" (*rappresentanza*): that by which every person is the bearer of an inalienable right, insofar as every life is measurable only in relation to itself. This is the theme of the person's "inalienability." The equality of rights, which currently is willfully confused with the equality of individuals, is born from this assumption. It does not appear to me that feminist thought has addressed this yet. Within the limits of an article like this, I think I can say that this is a key point, and it is founded on the "neutrality" of the citizen as the basic component in the formation of the wills: universal suffrage. This is precisely what all critiques from the right and from the left are not able to tarnish credibly without reducing the individuals—perhaps pro tempore, as in the thesis of the proletariat dictatorship—to rulers and ruled, with fundamentally unequal rights. In citizenship, every "difference"—of sex, race, religion, age, or status—is a power difference.

The contract of the "polis" is, in fact, abstract: at the founding moment of democracy, the citizen is neutral. If such has not been the case, it is because of the tendency of the strongest to retain their right of citizenship by sex, or by money or by origin. This neutrality must however be safeguarded. Even for the sake of tearing down the subsequent "non-neutrality" of the institutions in which, with universal suffrage in place, men have de facto participated, while reducing women, for the most part, to pure and simple voters. This process needs to be examined in its constitution and its possible dissolution.

And, here, there are two paths. One is that by which women, in carving out their identity and, thereby, the specificity of their "(ideal) representation" (*rappresentazione*) through "difference," make use of "(political) representation" (*rappresentanza*) to obtain, within the institutions, a negotiating presence that is sufficiently strong to alter those rules and aspects of the legislation that fixes the sexual division of labor as "duties" or coercions. Such a legislation has thrown women into the sphere of social reproduction, the invisible work that consists not in making children but in raising them and guaranteeing to their fathers, to the fathers' fathers, and so on, a place of replenishment (relaxation, food, ablutions, assistance) of their strength, in addition to the reassuring terrain of men's interior identity (the family as a maternal womb).

This division of labor, which has passed from early civilizations to our own, has shaped that work—invisible because it is not "monetized"—that not only constitutes the double work of the "working" woman, placing her from the start in a position of market inferiority: but it has also shaped our "material civilization." The type of house, of clothes, of city, of consumption, all the services we often speak of while rarely asking what needs they respond to, are drawn on the hidden screen of millions of women who clean, wash, iron, cook, buy, stand in line, and substitute for the times and performances of others.

The other path is that of separating oneself from the "polis" in order to establish a principle of "visibility" that is entirely external to the existing forms of "(political) representation" (*rappresentanza*), and from here elaborate a different politics, a different order of general social relations. This is also, but not only, "a different way of being in politics," as put forward by the theories of "entrustment" or of the "pact among women"— theories that are essentially constitutive of a subject that is helped in identifying herself, in not fading by weakness or tiredness into the styles of the other sex. But this path defers approaching the complex nature of state and social relations and leaves women to be suspended between "estrangement" and "being at ease in social interactions." And it takes it as a given that simply being within or close to such social interactions, being visible instead of invisible, would substantially modify their nature through a symbolic impact.

It goes without saying that this second path eliminates (political) representation (*rappresentanza*) as secondary or obsolete, privileges (ideal) representation (*rappresentazione*), and gives itself a long time. To its advantage is the tendency that is currently present within almost all structured societies, that is to say, a stronger pressure exercised by molecular processes than the one in the past. To employ Luhmann's pattern, if powers remain in a separate sphere where a political market occurs in relation to a base that is essentially used as a place for testing consensus, but that neither mandates nor is capable of controls, then the current trend would show that this base, which is no longer the domain of strong social-political subjects, nevertheless is not a silent and powerless assemblage, to which the established powers only suggest: "you single, or you group, try to become one of us." It is an educated and restless base, not gregarious, and about to change what immediately surrounds it. In short, it is able to slowly undermine power structures that are apparently invincible.

It is probable that these two processes can find a combination. But for the women who accept "(political) representation" (*rappresentanza*) and for the parties that include them in their lists of candidates, a problem presents itself, which was less urgent before: how to help the process of "(ideal) representation" (*rappresentazione*) while making use of the institutions, and how to make use of the legislating power to modify the material, and juridical structures in which woman is inserted from birth. After all, this would be nothing else than a process of blunt and complete emancipation, of which one wrongly says that there has already been too much: in fact, it is still very scarce.

There is no doubt that in this way, parliamentary women will clash with their own parties. For to preserve, within the "protection of the family," the entire sexual reproduction of roles is constitutive, for example, of the Christian Democratic Party's image of the state and of society. In fact, such a party has acted essentially in terms of laws of "protection" (*tutela*) that tend to "facilitate" the invisibility of women's work instead of making it visible, accounting for it, and desexualizing it. But this idea has infiltrated the left as well, because the alternative implies a social revolutionizing of the state, from culture to state budget, of welfare (which has never been thought from the perspective of the two sexes), and of services. No one, for now, proposes or addresses any of this.

How much does a certain feminism conform to this as well? The one that treasures the "specific" in what we have always been, giving it a sign of value instead of nonvalue. But this is a linchpin of its own self-rethinking for a "gender" that has historically been shaped into a role, that sees itself critically, but that struggles to get rid of such a role because it fears exiting itself and becoming just like the other sex, and nothing more.

Yet this internal limit is perhaps the easiest one to overcome, as soon as women acquire a "political" identity and a consistency that are strong and manifest. To acquire them, women have, alas, to cross in a short time the entire politological tradition, which is many centuries old, to revisit it from the perspective of a bisexed society, to choose what needs to be destroyed, destroy it . . . and to impose another order. It will not be a painless war. But is it a worthy challenge.

Care Amiche[5, 6]

It seems that it is not possible to get near feminine thought or, actually, *feminine*[7] thoughts, without arousing reactions of appropriation or refusal, like during the good old times of cliques. This goes to show that the "political" is hard to change in its orders of deployment, belonging, loyalty, or disloyalty. And women's thought is truly "political," and it is such not only when it affirms to be "politics" tout court, meaning that whoever does not go through its elaboration is politically already dead. The repeated announcement of the end of feminism is proof of this also. Only what is unsettling is exorcised.

But I would like to see up close, and starting from the stigmata of my age and my Marxist and communist formation, the features or the aporias of this form of being political (*politicità*). Almost all the women who write about women come from my side, from the ribs of the left; the feminism of the Radical Party[8] has perhaps been the last word of emancipation. The *feminine* texts of the 1970s, however, detach themselves from emancipation; they give but a reductive representation of it, because they fear the temptation of competing with men, of accepting their horizon. This is the limit they have seen in the old left and the new left, which is political and trade-union oriented, even in the most revolutionary left; therefore, from the initial "consciousness of being exploited" to the attempt of a fruitful contamination with the PCI (Partito Comunista Italiano)[9] through the Charter of Women, they have only accumulated proofs of an impossibility. From a distance, the most interesting connection appears to be that with the 1968 antiauthoritarian movement, which searches for the roots of power within the most intimate aspects of the person, but stops at the threshold of the uneven male/female relationship. It is the feminists who unveil the authoritarianism of the antiauthoritarian male, and who ask themselves about the internalization of authoritarianism that women have undergone up to now. This is the "different," the *feminine* step, so scorching that it will remain alive and unscathed by the *riflussi*[10] of old and new parties and movements.

This is something that even someone like me has understood, someone who has always asked herself about the "woman condition" but not about the *feminine* as a specificity and not a lack, as a being and not a "being not yet"—precisely, the difference. And this difference emerges after a millennium-old codification of language and the social orders that has been achieved in the presence of two sexes, yet with the values and the words of only one. He thinks for both, fixating the female sex in the role of the custodian of sentiments and primary reproduction yet aphasic in the realms of reason and social reproduction.

But how does the "authentic *feminine*" emerge? The answer that we have been given is: from an interrogation of depth experiences (*il profondo*), from a finally nonmediated "starting from oneself." To say it with the words of Lea Melandri, from the originary regions of the relationship between male and female, in the "intersection between nature and culture, nature and history." To say it with the words of Lia Cigarini, from the perception of an "uneasiness" in being in the code of others, from the need "to make our body, our sexuality speak." The region of sexuality is dark, both as a direct experience and as a totalitarian projection of the manly onto what is thought and is socially decided. Sexuation and sexuality—different declensions of a kernel where what we habitually define as body and mind intersect. Intriguing are both the body and the mind; they are, actually, the one that is interrogated by depth analysis.

A strange journey that of this *feminine* thought, considering that the fathers of psychoanalysis are men who are strongly anchored in the system of male values. Freud hesitates between a feminine that appears to him as lack and a feminine that opposes him as a dark continent. Yet *feminine* thought goes through Freud and Lacan, and less so—it seems to me—through Melanie Klein. The fact that two teachers of the patriarchal symbolic order have provided the *feminine* with a fundamental crowbar is proof of how complicated the pathways of formation are.

But the crowbar is not only theoretical: it is a modality of knowing. There is a difference between having understood the asymmetry of bodies and of cultures through a reading of Irigaray's *This Sex Which Is Not One* or through the practice of *autocoscienza* (consciousness raising). In the first modality there is a defense, a distance that mitigates what, in the youngest women, has been a suffering, a choice of destiny, a conflict, carried out within one's interiority and in the relationship with the other.

And what are the political outcomes of this? Those who are most interested in *autocoscienza* (consciousness raising) and in the movement that comes from it (a combative alterity that is visible also in the public squares), hold as central the interrogation of the masculine and the feminine as modalities that are both archetypical and intertwined in multiple ways, and conflicting in every individuality, so that the reflection on the historical and social order appears overdetermined from the origins, a pattern in perpetual movement and return. Considered from the outside, as it happens to me, the limit of this research lies in the difficulty of transitions from the archetype to concrete historicity and the present, because this approach tends to highlight what remains self-identical and to lose the reasons, and even the margin, as Gramsci would say, of the autonomy of historical forms. This attitude belongs precisely to the psychoanalytical approach, wherein what is common and recurring holds the central stage and becomes the explanation for the singular and the transient.

Different is the outcome of those who aim at defining an originary difference, intact and capable of its own cultural projection that would be, as it were, absolute. A "*feminine* desire" that reorganizes world priorities by proposing itself, if an oxymoron is permitted, as a partiality that wants itself as a total method. But, I feel like objecting, how could an integral *feminine* subjectivity be born, within the total symbolic order of patriarchy, without having unfolded or intersected with the complex making of civilizations? There is here a resurgence of the metaphysical in the most ancient, if not premodern, sense of the term, which, not by chance, projects itself into the proposal of a symbolic order, such as that of a maternal genealogy, analogous to that of the law of the father. This occurs through a hierarchy renamed disparity, an authority called authoritativeness (*autorevolezza*), and a dependence called entrustment. This lexicon counts, and so do the shifts of accents; yet who does not know the wonderful exchanges between the one and the other? Not to mention the slipping or trivialization—despite the intentions of the proponents—of "feminine desire" toward a simplistic reaffirmation of femininity as value, which is repetitive of ancient roles made strong by a secular elaboration, of women's virtues, of their being able to tie together instead of breaking up, of caring instead of wounding, of their inclination toward the emotional order instead of the logical one, of the refusal not only of serialities but also of equalities.

Both these approaches are, for me, problematic. The reason is precisely that I cannot disregard the viewpoint of second-wave feminism, and I think that such a viewpoint should act in depth on the social and civic relations. It is not ambition that turns me away; on the contrary. But it seems to me that, in general, with the exception of few individual women thinkers, these new texts by women short-circuit the import of our century either by their attributing historical impasses to eternal returns or by their adapting to approximate adjustments to the currently dominant forces. In other words, the crisis of our century appears to me to be bypassed both by the confrontation with the archetypes of power (those of the public and of the private scenes) and by the tout court affirmation of a failure of the modern opposed through the palingenesis of the *feminine* symbolic order. Now, the symbol is part of the "real" but does not exhaust it. There is a "real" that, even as inert, remains even when it is not, or not yet, thought; so much so that every language translates something that appears to it as given. This bond cannot be eliminated, except at the cost of either leaving a great part of the "real" unexpressed (which is, actually, what *feminine* thought reproaches the "political" for), or allowing the symbolic to flutter in a perpetual self-representation.

I am a daughter of this century's "real" that is made of the powers, forms of knowledge (*saperi*), institutions, and subjects that have fought on the intolerability of an unjust property order, and that have folded back into the dead end of an attempted and failed reversal. But at stake are the "material" conditions of freedom, even of *feminine* freedom. About this, the *feminine* texts I have mentioned tell me nothing, or almost nothing. They elude this node because it would be either further behind or further ahead of women's subjectivity; or because it would not even be, it is a false node. To me, even though I do not consider it exhaustive of the person's experience, it is surprising that it is cut off.

It is also suspicious. It is not an innocent fact that postmodernity abounds in the primacy of symbolic production, in a galloping flight from the fanciful heaviness and inertia of the "real" or from the betrayal of symbolic precedents that would allegedly have failed (presumably, because of a real that at some point messes them up). For the most part, what enters and exits women's words is a 1989 that is disembodied of, I will not say an analysis, but at least a serious description of its before and after; a 1989 that is reduced exactly to being the symbol of the failure of another symbol. When it is not recovered (and not only by feminine thought), within a praise for the primary community, what enters and exits is a "social relationship," a generic figure, that has been voided of the tragic aspects that social relations have assumed in the fights, defeats, formation, and destruction of subjects during the last one hundred years. What thus enter and exit are curious readings of materialism, in terms of a rediscovery of the materiality of the body or of goods, whereas for Marx, the "real material" lies in the relations among individuals in view of production, accumulation, and profit.

But this could be discussed. There remains, for me, the need for a *feminine* subjectivity that gives reasons to me as well, a woman among women, about the lacerations of modernity, of our current times. Also, through a way of listening that is a little bit freer from our respective affiliations.

Notes

Introduction

1. For a historical and sociological analysis of Italian feminism of these years, see Maude Anne Bracke, *Women and the Reinvention of the Political: Feminism in Italy 1968–1983* (New York: Routledge, 2014). For an anthology of critical writings produced by feminist collectives during the same period, see *Italian Feminist Thought: A Reader*, ed. Paola Bono and Sandra Kemp (Oxford: Basil Blackwell, 1991).

2. Carla Lonzi, "La donna clitoridea e la donna vaginale," in *Sputiamo su Hegel: La donna clitoridea e la donna vaginale e altri scritti* (Milan: Scritti di Rivolta Femminile, 1974), 102–103. Unless otherwise stated, all translation from Italian of citations from articles, essays, and books in this volume are the author's.

3. The law on divorce, law 898, was introduced in Italy on the 1st of December 1970. In 1974, a referendum was held on this law, and through it Italian citizens expressed their will to keep it. The law on abortion, law 194, was approved in May 1978 and a referendum held in 1981 showed strong support for keeping such a law. A reform of family law, law 151, was introduced in 1975 and gave equal moral and legal rights to both spouses, man and woman, within the family. Until then, the fascist civil code of 1942 established a hierarchal family structure with the man as the head, and the woman in a subordinate position.

4. The "150-hour courses" were introduced in Italy in 1973, the outcome of contractual negotiations by the trade unions, which gave workers the opportunity to pursue studies to obtain a degree, acquire a specialization, or more broadly to perfect one's educational formation. Workers were guaranteed up to 150 hours of studies in the arc of three years or less, to be devoted to studies of their choice. The "150 hours" were part of the workers' working hours and were paid. Lea Melandri taught courses offered as part of the "150 hours" and talks about this significant experience in the conversation included in this volume.

5. *Il Manifesto* is an Italian newspaper that was created by the initiative of some known intellectuals and journalists on the left, among them Rossana Ros-

sanda, Valentino Parlato, Lucio Magri, and Luigi Pintor. It was first created as a monthly review in 1969 and became a daily in 1971. It calls itself "communist" but remains independent and has maintained a critical position toward the Italian Communist Party. The Italian Communist Party was dissolved between 1989-1991 and became the Partito Democratico della Sinistra. *Il Manifesto* continues to be issued to this day.

     6. Rossana Rossanda, *La ragazza del secolo scorso* (Turin: Einaudi, 2005), 348.

     7. Rossanda, *La ragazza del secolo scorso*, 330.

     8. The Republic of Salò was the puppet fascist government Mussolini established after he was removed from power in 1943. It "ruled" in Northern Italy, backed by German troops, until the end of WWII.

     9. Rossanda, *La ragazza del secolo scorso*, 74.

     10. Rossanda, *La ragazza del secolo scorso*, 78.

     11. Carla Lonzi, "Let's Spit on Hegel," in *Italian Feminist Thought: A Reader*, ed. Paola Bono and Sandra Kemp (Oxford: Basil Blackwell, 1991), 57.

     12. Lonzi, "Let's Spit on Hegel," 59 (*emphasis added*).

1. The Memory of Our Body

     1. *Autocoscienza*, literally, "self-consciousness," is usually translated in English as "consciousness raising." It is the practice, within the women's movement, to gather in small groups and tell each other their experiences as women. It was a political tool to analyze the feminine condition and it has played a central role in the Italian women's movement of the 1970s.

     2. *Liceo* is a type of high school that prepares students for university studies.

     3. Melegnano is a town southeast of Milan.

     4. Elvio Fachinelli, "Masse a tre anni," in *Il bambino dalle uova d'oro: Brevi scritti con testi di Freud, Reich, Benjamin e Rose* (Milan: Feltrinelli, 1974), 171–181. Please note, the citations throughout this conversation reflect Lea Melandri's continual and relentless wrestling with texts and authors she has engaged with over the course of many years. Wherever possible, the specific bibliographical reference has been provided. Otherwise, only the author's name is provided in the text. Unless otherwise specified, the translation of all citations from Italian referenced by Lea Melandri, including her own books and articles, is mine.

     5. Fachinelli, "Masse a tre anni," 175.

     6. Fachinelli, "Masse a tre anni," 175.

     7. Elvio Fachinelli, Luisa Muraro Vaiani, Giuseppe Sartori, eds., *L'erba voglio* (Turin: Einaudi, 1971).

     8. Fachinelli, *Il bambino dalle uova d'oro*, 254.

     9. Extra-parliamentary groups were political groups that rejected the official parliamentary procedures and preferred direct participation involving the masses. In this way, they sought to bring about political change outside the existing insti-

tutions. They were particularly strong in Italy in the 1960s and 1970s at the time when the effectiveness of political representation was questioned. Some of them were Lotta Continua, Avanguardia Operaia, and Potere Operaio.

10. *L'erba voglio* 1.1 (July 1971). It is also included in *Il Desiderio Dissidente: Antologia della rivista "L'erba voglio" (1971–1977)* (Rome: DeriveApprodi, 2018), 121.

11. *Quaderni Piacentini* was a left-leaning quarterly periodical founded in 1962, in Piacenza, a town in the Emilia-Romagna region, from which it takes its name. It addressed political, cultural, and social issues of the time. Its publication ended in 1984.

12. Elvio Fachinelli, "Il deserto e le fortezze," *L'erba voglio* 1.1 (July 1971): 13–15, 14.

13. Lea Melandri, *Come nasce il sogno d'amore* (Milan: Rizzoli, 1988; Turin: Bollati Boringhieri, 2002).

14. Elvio Fachinelli, *La mente estatica* (Milan: Adelphi, 1989; 2009).

15. Pierre Bourdieu, *Masculine Domination*, trans. Richard Nice (Stanford: Stanford University Press, 2001).

16. Non Una Di Meno is an international feminist movement that started in Argentina as Ni Una Menos in 2015 in response to the violence against women, femicides and gender violence. It immediately spread across the world and in Italy as well.

17. Lea Melandri, *Love and Violence: The Vexatious Factors of Civilization*, trans. Antonio Calcagno (Albany: State University of New York Press, 2019). In Italian, *Amore e violenza: Il fattore molesto della civiltà* (Turin: Bollati Boringhieri, 2011).

18. National and International Reports are issued by EU.R.E.S., a European research-based group. According to the 2018 report on gender violence in Italy, the number of gender violence cases happening within the family increased again (+ 0.7%) with never such a high percentage of female victims (40.3%). See https://www.eures.it/sintesi-femminicidio-e-violenza-di-genere-in-italia/.

19. See note 18.

20. The "150-hour courses" (*i corsi delle 150 ore*) allowed workers to attend courses to pursue a diploma and/or improve their professional skills. It was the result of a long struggle by the trade unions, and it enabled workers to devote some of their working hours to educate themselves. One hundred and fifty hours was the maximum number of hours of study a worker was granted over the course of three years or less. These 150 hours were an integral part of their contract and were paid.

21. Affori-Bovisasca designates an area on the outskirts of Milan.

22. The books in question are: Paola Melchiori, ed., *Verifica d'identità: Materiali, esperienze, riflessioni sul fare cultura tra donne* (Rome: Utopia, 1987); *Off Screen: Women and Film in Italy*, ed. Giuliana Bruno and Maria Nadotti (London: Routledge, 1988).

23. Name of the street, in Milan, where the group used to meet.

24. Paola Melchiori, ed., *Verifica d'identità: Materiali, esperienze, riflessioni sul fare cultura tra donne* (Rome: Utopia, 1987), 42.

25. Melandri calls "experiential writing" (*scrittura d'esperienza*) the kind of writing that is closely connected to personal experience and that, unlike more educated and specialized types of writing, is spontaneous and raw. As she points out, this kind of writing is rooted in the experience of *autocoscienza* of the 1970s women's movement.

26. Lea Melandri, "Due anni di esperienza non autoritaria nella scuola media di Melegnano" (Two years of non-authoritarian experience in the middle school of Melegnano), in *L'erba voglio*, ed. Elvio Fachinelli, Luisa Muraro Vaiani, Giuseppe Sartori, 67–79.

27. Italian magazines with prevalently feminine readership. *Ragazza In* is a magazine created specifically for adolescent girls.

28. Sibilla Aleramo, *Diario di una donna: Inediti 1945–1960* (Milan: Feltrinelli, 1978). All citations in this section are taken from Sibilla Aleramo's *Diario*.

29. Lea Melandri, "L'infamia originaria," *L'erba voglio* 5.20 (March–April 1975): 18–21. It is also included in *Il desiderio dissidente: Antologia della rivista L'erba voglio (1971–1977)* (Rome: DeriveApprodi, 2018), 232–238.

30. Carla Lonzi, "Mito della proposta culturale," in Marta Lonzi, Anna Jaquinta, Moderata Fonte, Carla Lonzi, *La presenza dell'uomo nel femminismo* (Milan: Scritti di Rivolta Femminile, 1978), 141.

31. The writings in question refer to a particular Milanese group of *autocoscienza*, "sexuality and writing," which appear in *A zig zag*, a special issue, in 1978. They also refer to the experiential writings of the courses for/of women, at the Libera Università di Milano (LUD) and the writings in the periodical *Lapis: Percorsi della riflessione femminile* (1987–1997).

32. Lea Melandri attributes this statement to Marina Zancan at the conference on "ricerca e studi delle donne" (research and studies of/on women) held in Modena, in the spring of 1987.

33. Milan Women's Bookstore Collective, *Non credere di avere dei diritti* (Turin: Rosenberg & Sellier, 1987); in English, *Sexual Difference: A Theory of Social-Symbolic Practice* (Bloomington: Indiana University Press, 1990).

34. Lea Melandri, "Presentazione," in *Lapis: Sezione Aurea di una Rivista*, ed. Laura Kreyder, Lea Melandri, Maria Nadotti, Rosella Prezzo, Paola Redaelli (Rome: ManifestoLibri, 1998), 9–14, 10.

35. Johann Jakob Bachofen, *Myth, Religion, and Mother Right* (Princeton: Princeton University Press, 1992).

36. Libera Università delle Donne was founded in 1987. Its website has been active since 2002, http://www/universitadelladonne.it/.

37. *A zig zag: Scritti non scritti* (1978): 31.

38. "Karstic," *carsico* in Italian, describes a geological terrain that results from the excavating effect of underground water on soluble limestone. This landscape is found in the Eastern Alps in Northern Italy. Figuratively, it is used to describe something that acts in hiding and in depth and whose effects will show at a later time.

39. Lea Melandri, *Lo strabismo della memoria* (Milan: La Tartaruga, 1991), 9.

40. Otto Weininger, *Sex and Character* (London: William Heinemann/New York: G. P. Putnam's Sons, 1907).

2. "But I Am a Woman"

1. Luisa Muraro, *Guglielma e Maifreda: Storia di un'eresia femminista* (Milan: La Tartaruga, 1985); La signora del gioco (Milan: Feltrinelli, 1976); *Le amiche di Dio: Margherita e le altre* (Naples: Orthotes, 2014).

2. Luisa Muraro, *Lingua materna, scienza divina: Scritti sulla filosofia mistica di Margherita Porete* (Naples: D'Auria Editore, 1995); *Le amiche di Dio: Scritti di mistica femminile* (Naples: D'Auria Editore, 2001).

3. The beguines were a movement of women that started in the late Middle Ages all across Europe. Often, though not always, they lived in a large or small community similar to other religious orders, yet they were not a religious order. They presented a more flexible structure and this led, in some instances, to conflict with religious authorities.

4. Marguerite Porete, *Le mirouer des simplex âmes*, Corpus Christianorum C.M., LXIX (Turnhout: Brepols, 1986). The English translation, Marguerite Porete, *The Mirror of Simple Souls* (Mahwah, NJ: Paulist Press, 1993), is not used here as it is considered misleading by Luisa Muraro, just as all the modern translations of the Mirror are, in that they are based on the only French translation of the text that deviates from the Latin and English versions, both prior and closest to the original vernacular, apart from the language and translation. Robert E. Lerner, a renowned scholar in the field, has acknowledged Muraro's correct interpretation. See Robert E. Lerner, "New Light on The Mirror of Simple Souls," *Speculum* 85 (2010): 91–116, note 43.

5. Ellen L. Babinsky translates the passage in question as: "For I do not have anything which I love more than the one suffices me." See Porete, *Mirror of Simple Souls*, 112. As stated in note 4, Luisa Muraro contests this translation as misleading.

6. Luce Irigaray, *Sexes et parentés* (Paris: Les Éditions de Minuit, 1987). In English: *Sexes and Genealogies* (New York: Columbia University Press, 1993).

7. *Autocoscienza* is a term coined by Carla Lonzi for the practice of women gathering and talking among themselves, usually in small numbers, to give words to their experience as women. It is usually translated as "consciousness raising" for its obvious connection to similar practices in North America; however, the practice of *autocoscienza* played a much more crucial role in the Italian feminist movement and had a more lasting impact.

8. Clarice Lispector, *The Passion according to G.H.* (Minneapolis: University of Minnesota Press, 1988).

9. Ivy Compton-Burnett, *More Women than Men* (London: Eyre & Spottiswood, 1948).

10. Cesare Casarino, "Mother Degree Zero; or, of Beginnings," in *Another Mother: Diotima and the Symbolic Order of Italian Feminism*, ed. Cesare Casarino and Andrea Righi, trans. Mark William Epstein (Minneapolis: University of Minnesota Press, 2018), 303–320.

11. Michel Foucault, *Les mots et les choses: Une archéologie des sciences humaines* (Paris: Gallimard, 1966); in English, *The Order of Things* (London: Tavistock-Routledge, 1970).

12. The Diotima philosophical community was founded in 1983 at the University of Verona by a group of women philosophers influenced by Luce Irigaray's thought of sexual difference, among them Luisa Muraro and Adriana Cavarero.

13. *Istituto magistrale* is a type of high school in Italy that forms and prepares future teachers.

14. Luisa Muraro, *Diotima: il pensiero della differenza sessuale* (Milan: La Tartaruga, 1987); *Tre lezioni sulla differenza sessuale e altri scritti* (Rome: Edizioni Centro Culturale Virginia Woolf, Gruppo B, 1994); *L'ordine simbolico della madre* (Rome: Editori Riuniti, 1991), translated in English as *The Symbolic Order of the Mother* (Albany: State University of New York Press, 2017); *Diotima: Oltre l'eguaglianza. Le radici femminili dell'autorità* (Naples: Liguori, 1995).

15. Luce Irigaray, *Speculum: L'altra donna* (Milan: Feltrinelli, 1975); in English, *Speculum: Of the Other Woman*, trans. Gillian C. Gill (Ithaca, NY: Cornell University Press, 1985). *Questo sesso che non è un sesso* (Milan: Feltrinelli, 1978); in English, *This Sex Which Is Not One*, trans. Catherine Porter (Ithaca, NY: Cornell University Press, 1985).

16. DEMAU stands for Demistificazione Autoritarismo (Demystification of Authoritarianism), and in a second moment added the word *patriarcale*, becoming: Demistificazione Autoritarismo Patriarcale (Demystification of Patriarchal Authoritarianism). It was a collective founded by a small group of women, in 1966, in Milan. *Il maschile come valore dominante* was published by this group. *Manifesto di Rivolta Femminile* is a publication by another feminist collective, Rivolta Femminile, founded in 1970 by Carla Lonzi, Carla Accardi, and Elvira Banotti.

17. Luce Irigaray, *Sessi e genealogie* (Milan: La Tartaruga, 1989); in English, *Sexes and Genealogies*, trans. Gillian C. Gill (New York: Columbia University Press, 1993).

18. Luisa Muraro, *Maglia o uncinetto: Racconto linguistico-politico sulla inimicizia tra metafora e metanomia* (Milan: Feltrinelli, 1981).

19. Geneviève Fraisse, *La sexuation du monde: Réflexions sur l'émancipation* (Paris: Presses de Sciences Po, 2018).

20. Evelyn Fox Keller, *Sul genere e la scienza* (Milan: Garzanti, 1995). Originally published in English as *Reflections on Gender and Science* (New Haven: Yale University Press, 1985).

21. Massimo De Carolis, *Il paradosso antropologico: Nicchie, micromondi e dissociazione psichica* (Rome: Quodlibet, 2008). In English: *The Anthropological Paradox: Niches, Micro-worlds, and Psychic Dissociation* (New York: Routledge, 2018).

22. *Femmes, genre, féminismes en Méditerranée: Hommage à Françoise Collin*, preface by Geneviève Fraisse, texts and documents collected and presented by Cristiane Veauvy and Mireille Azzoug (Saint-Denis: Éditions Bouchène, 2014).

23. Libreria delle donne di Milano, *Non credere di avere dei diritti: La generazione della libertà femminile nell'idea e nelle vicende di un gruppo di donne* (Turin: Rosenberg & Sellier, 1987). In English: Milan Women's Bookstore Collective, *Sexual Difference: A Theory of Social-Symbolic Practice* (Bloomington: Indiana University Press, 1990).

24. Diotima, *Oltre l'uguaglianza: Le radici femminile dell'autorità* (Naples: Liguori, 1995).

25. Lia Cigarini, "Prendere scienza e forza da una fonte femminile," in *La politica del desiderio* (Parma: Pratiche Editrice, 1995), 131–142.

26. Mary Catherine Bateson, *Composing a Life* (New York: Atlantic Monthly Press, 1989), 105. In Italian: *Comporre una vita*, trans. Ester Dornetti (Milan: Feltrinelli, 1992), 89.

27. Giannina Longobardi, "Cambiamenti," in Diotima, *Il cielo stellato dentro di noi* (Milan: La Tartaruga, 1992), 227–238, 232 (translation mine). Luisa Muraro indicates that the book written by Diotima is the original source for the book *The Symbolic Order of the Mother* authored by her.

28. Marcel Gauchet, "La fin de la domination masculine," Le *Débat* 3.200 (2018): 75–98.

29. Elena Ferrante, *La Frantumaglia*, new and expanded edition (Rome: E/O Editions, 2016), 257. The citation is taken from the Italian edition, which is more extensive than the English edition. In English, *Frantumaglia: A Writer's Journey*, trans. Ann Goldstein (New York: Europa Editions, 2016).

30. Luisa Muraro, "The Symbolic Independence from Power," in *The Italian Difference: Between Nihilism and Biopolitics*, ed. Lorenzo Chiesa and Alberto Toscano (Melbourne: re.press 2009), 81–94.

31. Iris Murdoch, *Existentialists and Mystics: Writings on Philosophy and Literature* (New York: Penguin Books, 1999), 337.

3. An Imaginary of Hope

1. *Liceo classico* is a type of high school, in Italy, that prepares students for pursuing classical studies at the college/university level. Its curriculum focuses on the study of Latin and Greek, and the reading of classical texts in their original language.

2. The philosophical community Diotima was founded in 1983 at the University of Verona, by a group of women philosophers influenced by Luce Irigaray's thought of sexual difference. It organizes public seminars, lectures, and events, but philosophical research is conducted only among women. It issues its own philosophical journal and has published several books since its inception.

3. Adriana Cavarero, *In Spite of Plato: A Feminist Rewriting of Ancient Philosophy* (Cambridge: Polity Press, 1995). In Italian, *Nonostante Platone: Figure femminili nella filosofia antica* (Rome: Editori Riuniti, 1990).

4. Judith Butler, *Notes toward a Performative Theory of Assembly* (Cambridge: Harvard University Press, 2015).

5. Luce Irigaray, *Speculum: Of the Other Woman*, trans. Gillian C. Gill (Ithaca, NY: Cornell University Press, 1985); Luce Irigaray, *An Ethics of Sexual Difference*, trans. Carolyn Burke and Gillian C. Gill (Ithaca, NY: Cornell University Press, 1993).

6. Adriana Cavarero, *Relating Narratives: Storytelling and Selfhood* (New York: Routledge, 2000) is the English translation of *Tu che mi guardi, tu che mi racconti: Filosofia della narrazione* (Milan: Feltrinelli, 1997).

7. Cavarero, *Relating Narratives*, 41.

8. Cavarero, *Relating Narratives*, 44.

9. The expression "familiar sense of self" is discussed in *Relating Narratives* on pages 34–36. It does not do full justice to the original Italian expression *sapore familiare di ogni sé* (*Tu che mi guardi*, 49), which is connected to the sense of taste. *Assaporarsi*, in Italian literally meaning "to taste oneself," is rendered as "self-sensing." See *Relating Narratives*, 35.

10. Adriana Cavarero, *Inclinations: A Critique of Rectitude* (Stanford: Stanford University Press, 2016), originally published in Italian as *Inclinazioni: Critica della rettitudine* (Milan: Raffaello Cortina Editore, 2013).

11. Cavarero, *Inclinations*, 11.

12. Hannah Arendt, "Some Questions of Moral Philosophy," in *Responsibility and Judgment*, ed. and with an introduction by Jerome Kohn (New York: Schocken Books, 2003), 81.

13. Cavarero, *Inclinations*, 14.

14. Cavarero, *Inclinations*, 113. In the Italian text, 158.

15. Cavarero, *Inclinations*, 115.

16. Adriana Cavarero, *Stately Bodies: Literature, Philosophy and the Question of Gender*, trans. Robert de Lucca and Deanna Shemek (Ann Arbor: University of Michigan Press, 2002). In Italian, *Corpo in figure: Filosofia e politica della corporeità* (Milan: Feltrinelli, 1995).

17. Elena Ferrante, *Frantumaglia: A Writer's Journey* (New York: Europa, 2016), 347, 350.

18. Ferrante, *Frantumaglia*, 221.

19. Adriana Cavarero, "Ombre aristoteliche sulla lettura arendtiana di Marx," in *Hannah Arendt, Marx e la tradizione del pensiero politico occidentale* (Milan: Raffaello Cortina Editore, 2015), 142–162.

20. Adriana Cavarero, *Democrazia sorgiva: Note sul pensiero politico di Hannah Arendt* (Milan: Raffaello Cortina Editore, 2019). English translation: *Surging Democracy: Notes on Hannah Arendt's Political Thought* (Stanford: Stanford University Press, 2021).

21. Adriana Cavarero, *For More than One Voice: Toward a Philosophy of Vocal Expression*, trans. and with an introduction by Paul A. Kottman (Stanford: Stanford University Press, 2005). In Italian, *A più voci: Per una filosofia dell'espressione vocale* (Milan: Feltrinelli, 2003).

22. The "sardines' movement" was born spontaneously in November 2019, in response to right-wing populism. It filled the squares of Italian cities with thousands of people who came together to protest against empty political rhetoric. The Italian name *sardine*, in English "sardines," refers to being many and being tight, just like sardines.

23. Elias Canetti, *The Memoirs of Elias Canetti* (New York: Farrar, Straus and Giroux, 2000), 407, 484.

4. Selected Essays by Rossana Rossanda

1. This essay appeared in *Memoria rivista di storia delle donne* 19–20, 1–2 (1987): 118–124, with the title "L'impenitente emancipata." *Memoria* was a periodical issued by Rosenberg & Sellier from 1981 until 1991. It promoted the discussion of changes in the history of women from an interdisciplinary perspective. I wish to thank Rosenberg & Sellier for kind permission to reprint the essay in translation in this volume. I also would like to thank Maria Luisa Boccia for pointing out this essay to me.

2. In the Italian text, Rossanda mistakenly attributes the painting to Nathan Lothman, but it was the cubist painter Nathan Isaevich Altman who painted the portrait of Anna Akhmatova.

3. This article appeared in the newspaper *Il Manifesto*, on June 4th, 1987, with the title "Una bella sfida, un conflitto sicuro. Le donne e la polis." I wish to thank *Il Manifesto* for kind permission to reprint the article in translation in this volume.

4. Rossanda employs the terms *rappresentazione* and *rappresentanza*, both of which can be translated as "representation" in English. Both the Italian terms and their English translation are elusive and polyvalent: they have more than one meaning, which itself is indicative of the intractability of the idea of "representation." For the sake of making Rossanda's distinction visible, I have placed (ideal) before "representation" when translating *rappresentazione* and (political) before "representation" for *rappresentanza*. The former, *rappresentazione*, refers to the more abstract process of representation by which the emphasis is more on "the whole," a shared way of understanding that is presumed. The latter, *rappresentanza*, is more grounded in the concrete relation between institutions and voters and how to measure concrete political outcomes. This does not address the complexity of the question of representation but it makes the distinction in the original text apparent. The question of representation was highly debated in Italy during the 1960s and 1970s, and some political groups,

so-called *extra-parlamentari* groups—literally, outside of parliament—formed on the premise that they could not be "represented" in parliament. It is easy to see why it is also an issue debated by feminist groups, as this article shows.

5. *Care amiche* is the Italian for "dear (women) friends." Rossanda is specifically addressing her "female" friends in this piece. Given that the standard English translation, "dear friends," would either lose the feminine or be somewhat awkward, "dear (women) friends," I chose to leave the title in Italian.

6. This article appeared in the newspaper *Il Manifesto* on December 6th, 1996. I wish to thank *Il Manifesto* for kind permission to reprint the article in translation in this volume.

7. "Feminine" is the English translation of the Italian term *femminile* (singular) and *femminili* (plural). It is an ambivalent term that, in Italian, cannot be reduced simply to a biological dimension of the human, although it explicitly denotes the feminine sexual difference. In the context of this article, Rossanda employs this term to refer to the various forms of thought that emerged and developed out of the 1970s' women's movement that, in their different elaborations, highlight the specificity of being woman. To indicate the polyvalence of the term I have italicized it, even though it is not italicized in the Italian text.

8. Members of the Radical Party, a party on the left.

9. The Italian Communist Party.

10. *Riflusso* literally means "ebb" and it is the Italian word used to describe the political quietism that followed the political mobilization and activism of the 1970s.

About the Author

Elvira Roncalli is Professor of Philosophy at Carroll College, Helena, Montana. She has studied philosophy at the State University of Milan, in Italy. She received her PhD in philosophy from the Catholic University of Louvain-la-Neuve, in Belgium, with a dissertation entitled "Life of the Mind, Love of the World: The Crucial Role of Judging in Arendt's Thinking." She has published articles on Arendt, Cavarero, Muraro, and is coeditor with Silvia Benso of *Contemporary Women Philosophers: Stretching the Art of Thinking* (State University of New York Press 2021). Her research centers on questions investigating mechanisms and relationships of domination and the interplay between embodied subjectivity and living space, between power and violence, between agency and political recognition.

Index

150-hour courses, 7, 35, 36, 39, 41, 54, 175n4, 177n20
Abortion, 6, 39, 175n3
Akhmatova, Anna, 157, 158, 183n2
Aleramo, Sibilla, 42, 43, 56
Alterity, 84, 129, 135, 163, 171
Arendt, Hannah, 1, 80, 91, 99, 101, 115, 116, 119, 122–124, 126, 127, 130, 132–135, 139–142, 145–148, 150
Aristotle, 75, 83, 90, 113, 114, 119, 121, 136
Autocoscienza, 5, 21, 24, 28, 31, 40, 44, 45, 48, 50, 61, 81, 82, 87, 94, 95, 171, 176n1, 178n25, 179n7
Authority, 6, 7, 25, 28, 45, 46–48, 75, 78–80, 85, 97–102, 107, 166, 172
Authoritarianism, 24, 119, 170, 180n16
Autonomy, 27, 45, 134, 163, 165, 172

Bateson, Mary Catherine, 99
Biology, 54, 86, 89
Birth, 23, 30, 34, 39, 40, 44, 50, 54, 59, 76, 91, 96, 127, 133, 134, 138, 162, 169
Bourdieu, Pierre, 32
Butler, Judith, 93, 119, 123, 125, 137, 141, 142, 147, 148, 150

Care, 32, 34, 36, 46, 53, 59, 80, 82, 119, 133, 140, 143, 147, 148, 150
Cigarini, Lia, 30, 65, 76, 80, 98, 105, 171
Citizen(ship), 39, 59, 123, 159, 160, 166, 167
Civilization, 49, 50, 53, 74, 161, 166, 167, 172
Collective, 6, 7, 12, 24, 26, 33, 40, 44, 146, 175n1, 180n16
Collin, Françoise, 95
Conscience, 143
Consciousness, 30, 32, 33, 42, 46, 163, 164, 170
Consciousness raising, 5, 74, 81, 87, 94, 171, 176n1, 179n7

Democracy, 96, 104, 141–145, 147–149, 167
Dependence, 4, 7, 34, 50, 57, 68, 82, 83, 127, 158, 159, 162, 172
Dialogue, 9, 13, 61, 118, 125, 135
Differentiation, 27, 40, 49, 51, 54
Diotima (Philosophical Community), 6, 7, 81, 100, 102, 104, 116, 124, 125
Diversity, 28, 92, 93
Dominance, 34, 86, 102, 103
Domination, 3, 5, 8, 13, 27, 30, 32–34, 43, 45, 47, 50, 53, 57, 58, 91, 101, 114, 119, 127, 144, 159

Index

Dualism, 5, 25, 27, 47, 49, 50, 51, 58

Emancipation, 9, 32, 46, 48, 52, 54, 87, 88, 91, 94, 158, 169, 170
Entrustment, 96, 168, 172
Essentialism, 88, 90
Experiential writing (*scrittura di esperienza*), 8, 40, 41, 45, 55, 61, 177n25
Exploitation, 26, 30, 43, 56, 57, 78
Equality, 47, 48, 84, 87, 89, 91, 97, 98, 99, 107, 128, 167

Fachinelli, Elvio, 19, 24, 25, 27, 28, 31, 32, 40
Femininity, 50–52, 172
Ferrante, Elena, 103, 119, 123, 138, 139, 149
Foucault, Michel, 79, 119
Fox Keller, Evelyn, 92
Fraire, Manuela, 44
Friendship, 1, 14, 15, 28–30, 73, 96, 97, 125
Freedom, 23, 25, 27, 32, 33, 37, 47, 55, 59, 77, 82, 83, 86, 88, 92, 93, 96, 97, 105, 107, 122, 158, 173
Freud, Sigmund, 71, 75, 171

Gauchet, Marcel, 102
Gender, 2, 24, 27, 29, 30, 33, 45–54, 57, 58, 76, 89, 94, 101, 105, 116, 129, 148, 161, 164, 165, 169, 177n16, 177n18

Happiness, 8, 22, 36, 59, 76–78, 105, 142, 143, 146–148
Helpless(ness), 34, 135, 140
Heterosexuality, 49, 91, 92, 138
Homosexuality, 91, 92, 125, 138
Humanity, 49, 70, 90, 107
Humanism, 122, 123, 149

Identity, 47, 51, 53, 55, 90, 93, 130, 148, 164, 167, 169

Individual(ity), 8, 24–26, 28, 30, 33, 41, 43–46, 49, 54, 69, 78, 82, 86, 93, 102, 117, 118, 124, 126, 145, 160, 166, 167, 171, 173
Inequality, 128, 144, 145, 150
Irigaray, Luce, 72, 83–85, 88, 89, 104, 124, 126, 137, 163, 180n12, 181n2

Law, 4, 6, 7, 52, 78, 87, 90, 97, 102, 134, 160, 166, 169, 172, 175n3
Lesbianism, 55, 91, 97, 125
Levinas, Emmanuel, 119, 127, 130, 135, 136, 140
Liberation, 14, 27, 28, 32, 46, 48, 50, 53, 54, 58, 148, 157, 158
Lispector, Clarice, 74, 139, 149
Lived Experience, 30, 39, 40, 44, 45, 58, 81, 160, 164
Lonzi, Carla, 4, 13–15, 31, 44, 74, 84, 107, 179n7, 180n16
Love, 8, 22, 30, 33–35, 39, 42, 49, 53, 59, 60, 72, 73, 78, 97, 105, 127, 136, 143, 162

Man, 4, 5, 7, 8, 15, 25, 27, 28, 30, 32, 34–36, 42, 45, 47, 49–51, 69–71, 78, 84, 86–88, 96, 99, 118, 126, 136, 137, 158, 160, 161, 163, 175n3
Marx, Karl, 10, 141, 173
Masculine, 32–34, 41, 42, 47, 48, 50–54, 58, 86, 89, 91, 92, 102, 137, 164, 171
Masses, 23, 26, 31, 141, 142, 145, 176n9
Maternal, 49, 50, 52, 53, 92, 101, 126, 132, 133, 139, 140, 160, 167, 172
Monti, Adriana, 37
Murdoch, Iris, 107

Narrative, 7, 96, 119–122, 126, 138, 139, 141, 149, 150
Natality, 91, 122, 133, 134, 141, 148

Objectivity, 48, 69, 79

Oppression, 14, 26, 30, 43, 150, 158

Patriarchy, 32, 54, 57, 72, 75, 97, 100, 102, 128, 159, 172
Plato, 74, 113, 114, 119, 121, 123, 126, 132, 136–139
Plurality, 31, 55, 84, 91, 122, 124, 134, 141, 142, 143, 145–149, 151
Polis, 30, 39, 47, 50, 123, 165–168
Porete, Marguerite, 72, 87, 105, 179n4
Postmodern(ity)(ism), 114, 125, 129, 130, 132, 136, 173

Representation, 13, 42, 47, 50–52, 58, 133, 138, 165–168, 170, 173, 177n9, 183n4
Responsibility, 53, 56, 100, 130, 134–136
Reversal, 22, 46, 47, 173
Revolution, 31, 48, 97, 101, 102, 114, 128, 141, 164, 166

Self(hood), 76, 130–132, 135, 182n9
Separatism, 24, 27, 44, 124
Sexism, 30, 33, 35, 39, 43, 58, 88, 144
Sexuality, 21–23, 27, 29, 30–32, 34, 38, 39, 41, 43, 44, 46–50, 52, 57, 116, 162, 164, 171, 178n31
Story, 24, 26, 27, 29, 31, 37, 41, 45, 71, 80, 86, 90, 94, 96, 97, 102, 121, 130, 131, 137, 158, 162
Subordination, 7, 26, 91, 161

Symbolic, 5–7, 28, 31, 32, 44–49, 51, 55, 57, 69, 72–75, 77, 79, 80, 82, 84, 86, 88, 93, 94, 96–102, 118, 124, 133, 136, 139, 148, 150, 168, 171–173

Tradition, 32, 45, 69, 70, 81, 93, 101, 114, 115, 123–126, 128, 129, 138, 139, 161, 165, 169
Truth, 5, 10, 37, 47, 69, 75, 76, 79, 86, 107, 127, 138, 139

Unconscious, 6, 21, 28, 30, 39–41, 45, 48–50, 58, 162
Uniqueness, 91, 122, 124, 126, 130, 131, 134, 135, 137, 145, 146
Utopia, 26, 127

Value, 2, 6, 7, 47, 48, 50, 52, 54, 72, 84, 91, 94, 100, 103, 124, 127, 159, 162, 169–172
Violence, 11, 13, 21, 22, 32–35, 42, 44, 55–57, 78, 82, 87, 93, 140, 142, 150, 177n16, 177n18
Vulnerability, 127, 132, 134, 136, 140

Weil, Simone, 75, 91, 96, 101
Womb, 139, 160, 167
Woolf, Virginia, 42, 48, 53, 72, 104, 119, 120

Zamboni, Chiara, 102, 116

www.ingramcontent.com/pod-product-compliance
Lightning Source LLC
Chambersburg PA
CBHW021142230426
43667CB00005B/222